D0518080

ART CENTER COLLEGE OF DESIGN
3 3220 00261 5735

Santiago Calatrava

MILWAUKEE ART MUSEUM QUADRACCI PAVILION

The PFISTER
LEASE

Santiago Calatrava

MILWAUKEE ART MUSEUM QUADRACCI PAVILION

BY CHERYL KENT

FOREWORD BY DAVID GORDON

NEW COLOR PHOTOGRAPHY BY JEFF MILLIES, HEDRICH BLESSING

First published in the United States of America by Rizzoli International Publications, Inc.
300 Park Avenue South
New York, NY 10010
www.rizzoliusa.com

2005 2006 2007 2008 / 10 9 8 7 6 5 4 3 2 1

ISBN: 0-8478-2701-1 (cloth)
ISBN: 0-8478-2727-5 (paperback)

Library of Congress Control Number: 2004099807

Edited by Robert V. Sharp
Designed by Steve Biel, Milwaukee Art Museum

Printed in China

PHOTOGRAPHY CREDITS
All color photographs, except as noted below, were produced for this publication by Jeff Millies of Hedrich Blessing, Chicago.

Additional images were received from and are copyrighted by
James Auer, from his personal collection, reprinted with his permission: p. 49b
Jim Brozek: pp. 48, 49t, 54, 68t, 68b, 82t, 82m, 87b, 88, 89
Valerie Brzezinska: pp. 68m, 82b
Ezra Stoller © Esto: p. 66b
Heinrich Helfenstein: pp. 38bl, 47
Timothy Hursley: pp. 69, 90, 102, 103
Milwaukee Art Museum: pp. 30, 33, 106
Paolo Rosselli: pp. 37b, 38t, 38br, 40, 43,72

Frontispiece: View east down Wisconsin Avenue, through downtown Milwaukee, toward the Milwaukee Art Museum

Contents

7 Foreword
DAVID GORDON

23 Winged Victory: The Milwaukee Art Museum
CHERYL KENT

104 Project Personnel: Milwaukee Art Museum, Quadracci Pavilion

107 Project Drawings: Plans, Elevations, and Sections

114 Santiago Calatrava: Biography

122 Santiago Calatrava: Selected Projects and Works

124 Selected Bibliography

127 Acknowledgments

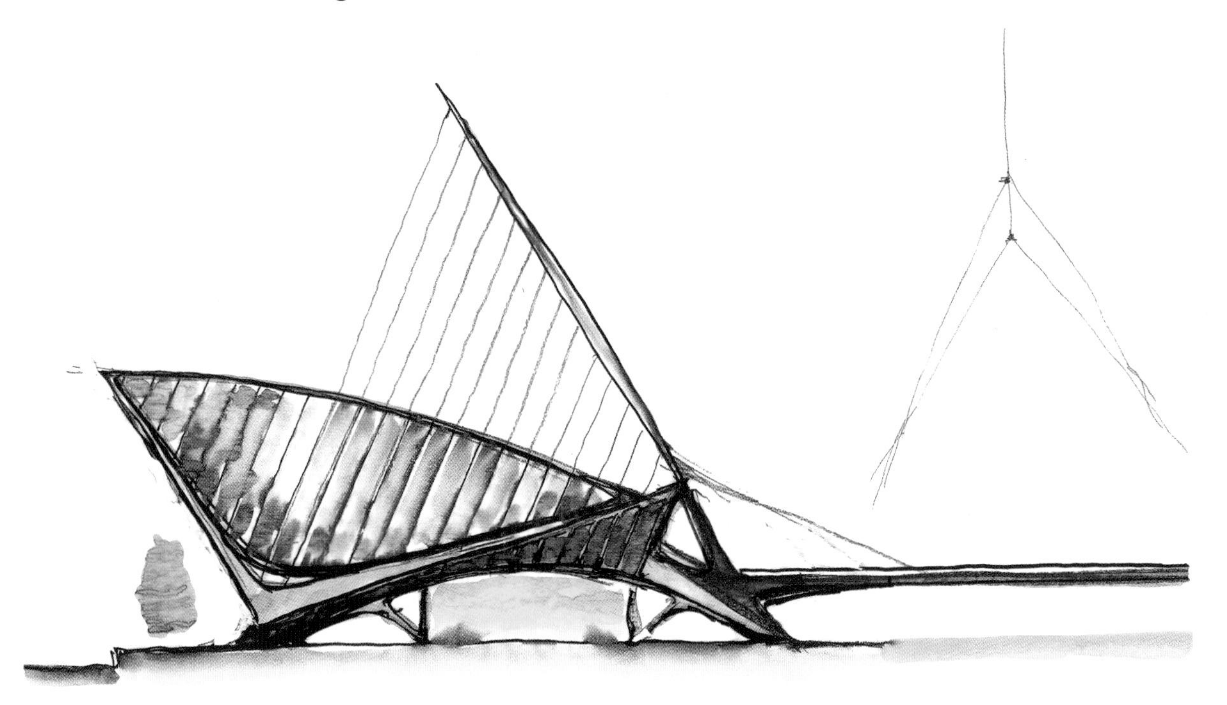

Preliminary sketch of the Milwaukee Art Museum addition, 1995.

Foreword

It was love at first sight. As I walked from my hotel east along Wisconsin Avenue, a great white structure at the end of the street—set against blue sky and a blue lake—filled me with excitement. I had come from London to be interviewed for the directorship of the Milwaukee Art Museum. When the call first came about the position, I had not known about the Calatrava-designed Quadracci Pavilion. The official opening had taken place a month after 9/11, and the world's attention was elsewhere. I knew Milwaukee only vaguely, but that it was the site of Santiago Calatrava's first U.S. building certainly got my interest. How could this city have pulled off such a coup? So I came. I saw. I was conquered.

What I saw was a sculpture. A work of art with allusions, metaphors, poetry. The wings of a giant mechanical bird seemed to be lifting the building up and away over the lake. The suspension bridge suggested weightlessness. The soaring reception hall, with its bright light and reflective white marble floor, was the nave of an ethereal cathedral. Its glass-faced prow was the bow of a boat but also the snout of an open-mouthed shark. The ribs down the gallerias made spinal skeletons. My reaction was that of nearly everyone who encounters the building: a spiritual uplift—or, to quote most visitors, "Wow!" The sense of awe and wonder does not diminish. The varied lake climate creates a constantly changing light show.

Burke Brise Soleil seen from beneath Mark di Suvero's *The Calling* (1982) in O'Donnell Park.

Architecture has always been important to me. In London I was lucky enough to have worked in buildings designed by distinguished architects: The Economist Building (Peter and Alison Smithson, 1959–64), the Independent Television News headquarters at 200 Gray's Inn Road (Norman Foster, 1988–90), and the Burlington House home of the Royal Academy of Arts (Colen Campbell and Lord Burlington, 1717–20, and others before and since). My late brother Max had been both an architect and a collector of contemporary art. He had been burdened with me as a grumpy teenager on a road trip in France in the 1950s. We went to Le Corbusier's Ronchamp chapel on a rainy day, and I was impressed by the waterfall created by a spout on the roof that the architect had arranged for such a day as that. My eyes were opened to the exciting possibilities of architecture.

Max was a minimalist. His memorial exhibition at the Architecture Foundation in London was called *No Trim*, a title that summed up his views on art, architecture, people, and things. He had worked on many spaces for artists and collectors. He was responsible for the first Saatchi Gallery on Boundary Road, St. John's Wood, London. He designed the Manilow House in Chicago. It was only after his death in 1990 that I became part of the art world that he had long inhabited, becoming chairman of England's Contemporary Arts Society and a trustee of the Tate Gallery. He had a great influence on my aesthetic judgment, and I miss the opportunity of getting his views on art and architecture. I have to make do with conversations with him in my head.

How would minimalist Max with his rectilinear disposition and his love for Bauhaus lines have responded to the zoomorphic shapes of Calatrava? One visiting museum director had scathingly described the building as what a science fiction illustrator in the 1950s would have drawn as a space station. But I think Max would have loved many aspects of this museum: its clean white lines, even though they curve; the subtlety of the long low building that creates a breathing space between Eero Saarinen's 1957 original structure and Calatrava's arresting addition; the pure space of Windhover Hall; the decision to make the parking garage both dramatic and, more practically, warm for the Wisconsin winter; the sheer unbridled exuberance of the Burke Brise Soleil; and, finally, the unfailing attention to detail and quality. He would also have appreciated the fundamental integrity of the building: it is a visionary piece of architecture carried out with an engineer's economy of effort. Sensational the building may be, but of trim there is none.

Santiago Calatrava is a rare combination. Of architect and engineer. Of artist and mathematician. Of knowledge and imagination. He has Spanish passion (from the country where he was born) and Swiss control (from the country where he was educated and married). He does freehand watercolors of dancing people and he makes precise sculptures that rely on careful calculation of balance and tension not to fall down. The museum is considering an exhibition of his watercolors and sculptures to be called *Left Brain/Right Brain* because he has the power to imagine and the expertise to build what his creativity has invented.

The Quadracci Pavilion is a work of art. But then architecture is the most public and permanent of the arts, and it is a great pity that so little of it aspires to be art. There is much discussion about new museum architecture, and the great sin understandably is for the architecture to dominate the art. That is not the case at the Milwaukee Art Museum. Entering the Calatrava heightens one's visual sense and predisposes visitors to appreciate the art they are about to see. It was notable that Victoria Newhouse, whose influential book *Towards a New Museum* takes a critical view of many new museums, admired Calatrava's skillful siting of the pavilion and its engineering pyrotechnics. The building is also effective in use. The central (Baker/Rowland) gallery is a large rectangle without obstructions that has proved very flexible for a wide range of temporary exhibitions. The Schroeder Galleria to the west is used to display a site-specific work of art each year and the Baumgartner Galleria to the east is the sculpture-filled artery leading to the permanent collection. It is top lit so that natural light can soften artificial light. Admission to Windhover Hall—the great nave—and to the store and the café is free: we want members of the community to feel proud of the building and to show it off to friends and family without having to buy a ticket. Windhover Hall is used for opening receptions, concerts, memorial services, grand dinners, workshops, and, yes, it can be rented for private events. The store, with gorgeous fixtures designed by Calatrava, has become established as an upscale shop. The café,

with its inviting outlook toward Lake Michigan, is becoming a destination in its own right. The Lubar Auditorium, with seats designed by Calatrava, has excellent acoustics for lectures and is also used for showing movies.

Max was due to give a lecture about the architecture of museums before he died. He was too ill, however, and Richard Serra gave the lecture from notes by Max. The point he made was that while a museum is primarily a place for preserving and displaying art, a museum visit is an experience of which the art is but one part, and museums have to address the needs of the demanding modern visitor for that experience to be a satisfying one. Our building passes the test.

I have had the good fortune to inherit a building that I love. The agony of constructing it fell to others, and I pay tribute to the former presidents—Allen Samson, Mike Mahoney, Jack Pelisek, and Donald Baumgartner—and the former director and executive director—Russell Bowman and Christopher Goldsmith—and the Building Committee Members (p. 104) who were conscious of building a masterpiece and did not curtail the architect's vision. Indeed *Building a Masterpiece* is the title of the book that was published in 2001 when the building opened. It covers both the building and the museum's wonderful collections, but since that book had to go to press before the building was completed, we felt that it was important to do a new monograph with new photography.

I am grateful to the collaborators who have created this new book. In particular I am grateful to Cheryl Kent, who has written a superb essay filled with the enthusiasm of someone fortunate enough to have spent time with Santiago Calatrava, and to Robert V. Sharp, editor and project manager, who shaped the wood and sharpened the trees. I also applaud Jeff Millies and Bob Shimer of Hedrich Blessing, the noted Chicago-based architectural photography firm, for the lasting body of images Jeff created of this building; Steve Biel, the museum's gifted designer; and my former colleague Britt Salvesen who helped launch this project. In addition, I wish to acknowledge the work of two other members of our publications committee, Gwen Brenner and Martin Sovik, who was our principal liaison with our publishing partners, Rizzoli—in particular, David Morton, Charles Miers, and Ron Broadhurst—as well as our building engineer Chuck Loomis and Jonathan Lawson of our Prints, Drawings, and Photographs department. We are extremely grateful to well-known Milwaukee photographer Jim Brozek, Valerie Brzezinska of C. G. Schmidt, and art critic James Auer of the *Milwaukee Journal Sentinel* for the use of their photographs taken throughout the very difficult construction phase of this remarkable project. Finally, I want to express my thanks to Santiago and Robertina Calatrava and the Calatrava staff in Zurich for all their generous assistance in compiling a monograph on this singularly extraordinary architectural masterpiece.

DAVID GORDON, DIRECTOR AND CEO
MILWAUKEE ART MUSEUM

View, looking north,
of the Quadracci Pavilion and
Burke Brise Soleil.

Burke Brise Soleil and
South Wing and Terrace.

FOLLOWING PAGES
View, looking northeast, across
Lincoln Memorial Drive.

3 TONS OR OVER
MICHIGAN ST
Magnetic North
PARKING ENTRANCE

Winged Victory: The Milwaukee Art Museum

CHERYL KENT

On a clear June day just after noon, the white wings of the new addition to the Milwaukee Art Museum lift slowly against a blue sky. The building is often likened to a great bird, and the resemblance is never closer than when the last pieces of the wings move slowly into place. It looks as if the bird just shrugged, and straightened its spine preparing to fly off.

People assemble to watch the spectacle just before noon. It's a hot day and they are wearing shorts, T-shirts, flowered summer dresses, hats, and sandals, and a few of the older ones are wearing socks with their sandals. They carry cameras. Other people are dressed in the palette of black and gray that betrays the arts and architecture crowd, the cognoscenti of contemporary trends. All of them have come—some farther than others—to see one of the most dramatic and well-executed buildings constructed in America in years.

This building moves people. It is that rare thing, a new experience at the scale of a building. Even those who know what the building looks like and know that it involves motion are taken by the physical surprise of it. It is ethereal, completely white and connected to the older existing museum complex by a low, block-long gallery that culminates at the south end in a new entry for the museum and an immense new hall that is crowned by a peaked brise soleil, a movable louvered sunscreen. A cabled bridge connects the museum's front door with Milwaukee's business center, resolving in one gesture the isolation that has been the museum's chronic problem. The setting adds drama; it stands on the shore of Lake Michigan, which is vast and beautiful and offers no impediments to viewing the building.

To see the brise soleil in operation for the first time must be what it was like to have been at the World's Columbian Exposition of 1893 in Chicago when the world's first Ferris wheel turned, or to have seen the Eiffel Tower in 1889 when it was just completed, or to have been at the unveiling of Eero Saarinen's Gateway Arch in St. Louis in 1963. The museum addition has that combination of technological muscle and unlikely beauty that captivates people.

Milwaukee Art Museum director David Gordon is right when he says, "It is impossible to be pessimistic in this building." The addition is the image of optimism and delight. It evokes pleasure in the way the sculptures of Jean Tinguely and Alexander Calder do.

Up until now, Milwaukee has looked like an unassuming city with its conservative, safe architecture. In recent years, however, the loss of industry—the city's heritage—and the slow swing to a service economy have been a worrying preoccupation. At a time when Milwaukee needed a win, it got the museum addition and the world attention it inspired. It is not too much to say that the success of this project has brought a new spirit to the city, one that is more optimistic, more confident of the future, more willing to experiment. Since the completion of the museum's addition, a modern new high school has been constructed and the city has built a civic highway bridge that had been stalled because the architect wanted to do a contemporary design rather than the historical one the county preferred, or the generic, off-the-shelf version favored by state transportation engineers. This new bridge is resoundingly modern and clearly influenced by the cable-stayed bridges of the museum's architect, the Spanish-born Santiago Calatrava.

View, looking east, inside Windhover Hall.

The fierce desire to reinvent the image of an ageing, second-tier American city powered everyone involved in the museum project: from the trustees who raised the money for it to the construction workers who built it. In a curious turn, that passion may have made Milwaukee the one and only place in the United States where a building like this could have been built as beautifully as it was. Extraordinary demands were made of everyone and nobody wanted to fail.

Certainly Calatrava was partly responsible for this turnabout. He helped Milwaukee see itself in a new way. In Milwaukee, Calatrava saw a magnificently sited city, youthful by European standards and full of possibilities: "Milwaukee is like a teenager; Paris is an old lady. If you build in Paris it doesn't change very much. [In Milwaukee] it is possible to deliver a tremendous identity. It means your time is very important for this city."

Calatrava, who won the commission from a field of fifty-five architects in 1994, soon had Milwaukee's key citizens seeing their city and their museum addition as he did, potentially glorious. They had the site; they could build a masterpiece. The museum's trustees, who earlier had halved the project's scope and budget, reconsidered that decision and broadened the project beyond its original parameters. Calatrava would give them everything he had, flying to Milwaukee forty times over the course of the project. His design evolved into a very challenging building, full of curves requiring painstaking custom work and features that had never before been made for a building. The construction team, the managing architect, the engineer—the firms that hammer out the details and build the architect's design—were all Milwaukee companies, and none of them had ever worked on a building of such complexity, but together they produced architecture of surpassing craftsmanship and refinement. For everyone involved, it mattered very much that the project succeed and the world pay attention to what had been built in Milwaukee.

Calatrava was hardly unknown before this commission and he continued his ascent, rising to the ranks of the world's most sought-after architects once the Milwaukee Art Museum project was completed. Significantly, however, the addition to this museum offered Calatrava one of his first opportunities to incorporate movement at a large scale into one of his buildings, something that had fascinated him since graduate school. After the Milwaukee Art Museum, Calatrava won the job to design the Olympic Sports Complex (2001–4) in Athens, Greece, which also involves massive moving elements. He has also been selected to create the new World Trade Center Transportation Hub in Lower Manhattan, scheduled for completion in 2009. His addition to the Milwaukee Art Museum is perhaps one of his most satisfying built works, drawing on every discipline he values: urbanism, art, engineering, sculpture, and architecture as well as movement.

Skylight over Windhover Hall, with brise soleil open.

FOLLOWING PAGES
View, looking southeast, of the Quadracci Pavilion and Burke Brise Soleil.

Eero Saarinen,
Milwaukee County War Memorial and Milwaukee Art Center, 1957.

View, looking northwest, of the Milwaukee County War Memorial and Milwaukee Art Center, c. 1960.

THE BACKDROP

Expanding the Milwaukee Art Museum had been under discussion since 1988, even though a large addition that brought the facility from 20,000 to 140,000 square feet had been built just thirteen years earlier. Throughout the 1980s attendance was growing at the Milwaukee Art Museum, as was the public appetite for educational programs in the arts. But the museum did not have the facilities to support what museum-goers everywhere were coming to expect. The museum needed a gallery for special exhibitions, meeting rooms, a restaurant, a gift shop, and an auditorium. More than anything, however, Russell Bowman, the director, Christopher Goldsmith, the executive director, and the museum's trustees felt that the museum needed a stronger architectural identity.

The Milwaukee Art Museum's building addition fits in with a long list of recently constructed, architecturally daring museums and extensions that have determinedly cast aside the classical facades and Doric columns of old. Most conspicuous among these is the Guggenheim Museum (1997) in Bilbao, Spain, by Frank Gehry; but the list also includes more recent examples such as the Contemporary Arts Center (2003) in Cincinnati by the London-based architect Zaha Hadid; the American Museum of Folk Art (2001), New York, by Tod Williams and Billie Tsien of that city; and the de Young Museum (2005) in San Francisco by Swiss architects Jacques Herzog and Pierre de Meuron. Each of these institutions—and many, many more could be added to such a list—is intent on exercising architecture's power to attract and excite museum-goers within and beyond their city borders.

Before the new construction, the museum in Milwaukee—the original 20,000-square-foot building and its 120,000-square-foot addition—was a subdued complex of heavy stone and pink-tinted concrete. The first building was an early work by Eero Saarinen, the architect of two seminal 20th-century American structures: the TWA Terminal building (1962) at the John F. Kennedy Airport in New York, and the Gateway Arch in St. Louis. Saarinen's 1957 building combined functions for the Milwaukee County War Memorial and what was then known as the Milwaukee Art Center.
The first addition to the museum was finished in 1975 to accommodate the Bradley Collection, a gift of over 600 modern American and European works of art from Mrs. Harry Lynde (Peg) Bradley.
That addition was designed by David Kahler, a prominent Milwaukee architect from the firm Kahler, Slater & Fitzhugh Scott. Kahler deferred to the earlier structure out of respect for its function as a war memorial and out of regard for its architect. His addition was built low, partially nested beneath the cantilevered portion of Saarinen's structure and then extended east toward the lake. Through compatible geometry and massing and by matching the color of the concrete to Saarinen's original palette, Kahler blended the two buildings together. The galleries Kahler created are warm and enveloping, varying in scale, and they are particularly good for changing displays of modern art.

Both Saarinen and Kahler—as Calatrava would in his turn—grappled with the site's remoteness. The museum is built on landfill and is separated from downtown Milwaukee by distance as well as grade. The city's business and residential districts stand on Lake Michigan's original shoreline, a bluff more than four stories high and on the other side of the four-lane-wide Lincoln Memorial Drive from the museum. Until Calatrava addressed it, the problem had never been satisfactorily resolved.

Saarinen had hoisted the top story of his building up to the height of the bluff, in an attempt to address the issue, but with the building's massive stone walls at the landfill level and its deeply shaded windows—handsome as they are—it was as forbidding as a fortress. As a memorial, its brooding quality was appropriate, but it would be a problem for a museum that wanted to attract people and make art accessible. Kahler's addition could not soften the complex, but it would signal an important institutional shift of balance in favor of the museum.

View, looking northeast, of the Milwaukee County War Memorial and Milwaukee Art Center, with addition by David Kahler of Kahler, Slater & Fitzhugh Scott, 1975.

With an unmatched knowledge of the museum and nine years of service as a trustee, three of them as president, David Kahler, as president of Kahler Slater Architects, would work closely with Calatrava as the coordinating project architect—known formally as the architect of record—when the new addition was being designed and built.

For architects, museums are prized commissions. Most commercial projects are driven by cost and schedule. While these concerns are still present in the making of a museum, the architect also trusts that the client has taste, that aesthetics count and details will be appreciated, that the building will be well maintained and will stand for ages, and, finally, that architectural creativity has a chance of expression.

The selection of Eero Saarinen for the first building showed an institutional prescience in recognizing talent and a willingness to take a chance on it. A new generation of trustees wanted to do no less. Walter Annenberg, the former media magnate who was born in Milwaukee, gave a gift of $1 million in 1994 just to fund the architect selection process. An international invitation to architects was published, asking for submissions.

Because this new structure had to work with their existing museum, the trustees wanted an architect who could design within a modern idiom and who could demonstrate an ability to accommodate the concrete, steel, and glass that composed the bulk of the earlier structures. They wanted the new addition to include all the amenities their facility did not have, but most of all they wanted to raise the museum's profile through architecture. The committee of trustees who would make the final selection narrowed the number of candidates to ten.

These finalists made presentations in Milwaukee. One internationally famous architect sent

Preliminary sketches of the Milwaukee Art Museum addition, 1994.

Preliminary sketches of the Milwaukee Art Museum addition, 1995.

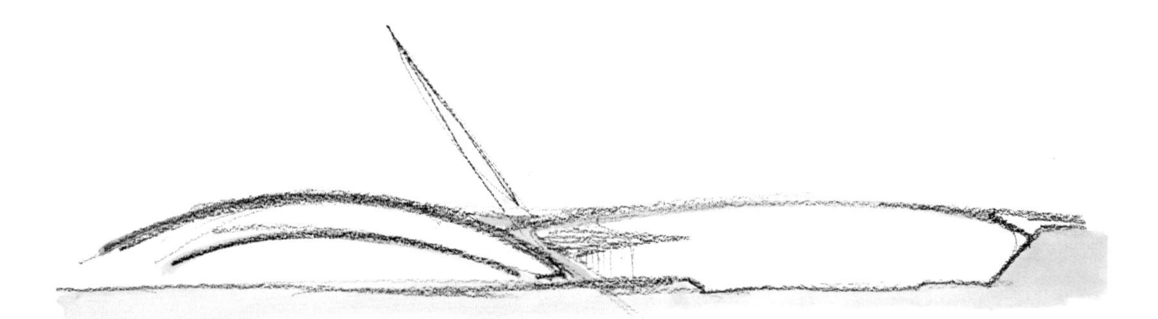

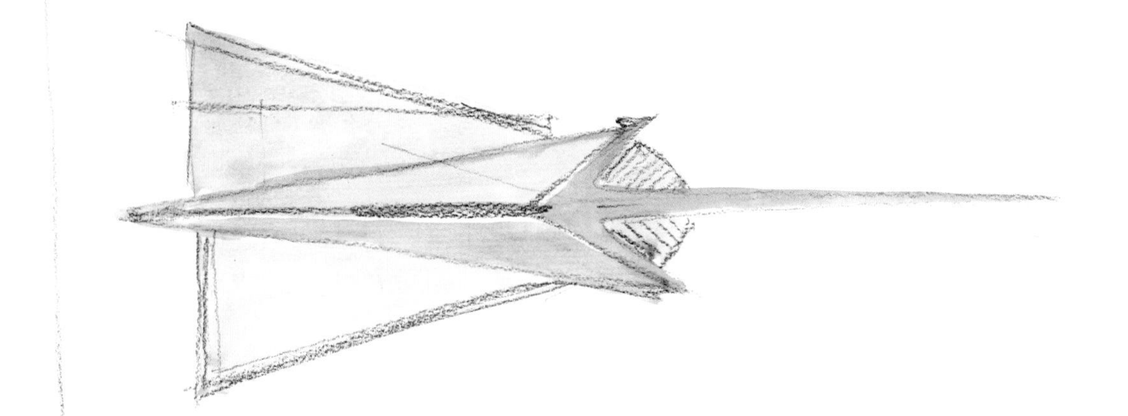

an associate instead of coming himself, raising hackles and anxiety among the trustees that their commission would not be taken seriously. Committee members debated whether they should choose a younger architect, one not yet at the peak of his career, just as Saarinen and Kahler had been when they worked for the institution. Such an architect, it was argued, would give the addition focused attention. Donald Baumgartner, a member of the selection committee—and subsequently chairman of the building committee and president of the museum's Board of Trustees—was an early enthusiast for Calatrava. He would not be disappointed.

Calatrava made a compelling presentation. While he speaks seven languages, he was uncomfortable about his English (he became nearly fluent in the course of the project). As he always does for client meetings and presentations, Calatrava carried watercolors, pens, markers, and paper. He pulled these from his briefcase the way a businessman might pull out a laptop with a PowerPoint presentation. While he talked, Calatrava painted and drew with amazing facility, explaining as he did so his work and his ideas to the trustees and museum directors. He was emerging as a favorite.

Traveling across the United States, to Japan, and to Europe, members of the selection committee, together with Russell Bowman, toured notable examples of the ten candidates' designs before making the final choice. As their plane descended to land in Lyon, France, Calatrava's Airport Railway Station (1989–94) came into view. A woman on the committee was looking out the plane's window at the steel-and-glass building below. She turned to Bowman, sitting beside her, and said, "I'm in love." That remark answered any question Bowman may have had: he was certain then who would be designing Milwaukee's new addition.

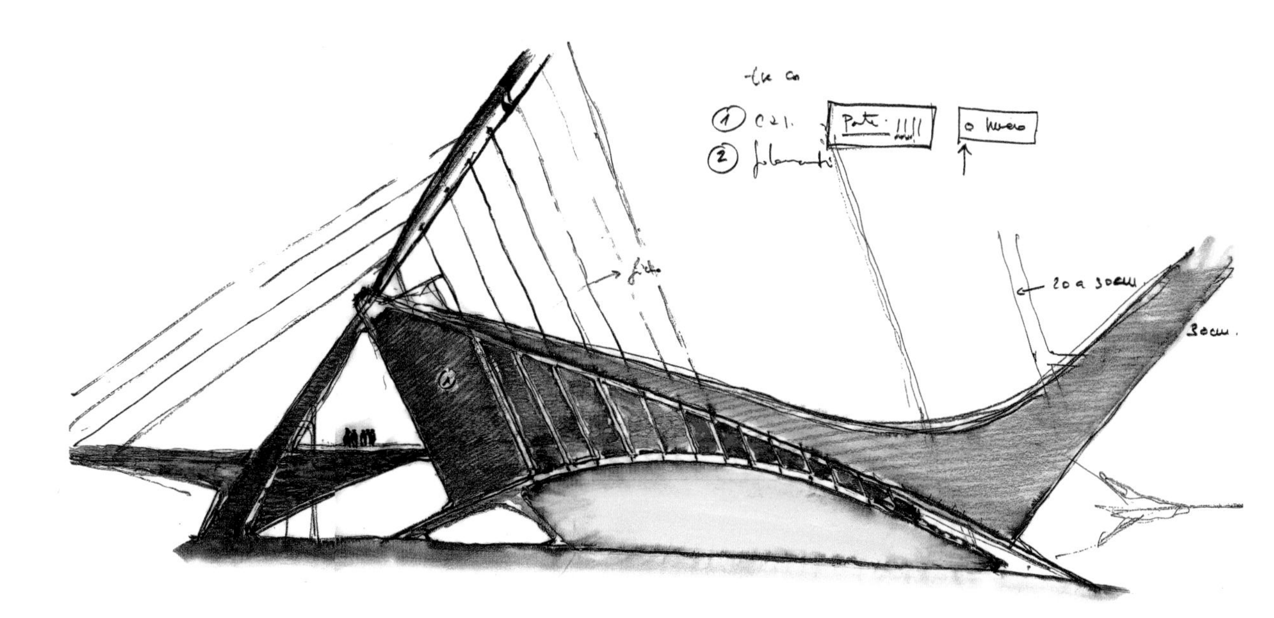

Preliminary sketch of the Milwaukee Art Museum addition, 1995.

Lyon Airport Railway Station, Satolas-Lyon, France, 1989–94.

Trinity Footbridge,
Salford-Manchester, England,
1993–95.

Kuwait Pavilion, Expo '92,
Seville, Spain, 1991–92.

Shadow Machine, installed at the
Museum of Modern Art, New York,
1993.

SANTIAGO CALATRAVA'S ARCHITECTURE

Calatrava is both an architect and engineer and when he speaks it is with a persuasive combination of passion and logic. He was born in Valencia, Spain, in 1951. He received his undergraduate degree from the Escuela Tecnica Superior de Arquitectura, Valencia. His undergraduate years were bracketed with formal study in two other subjects that also exert strong influences on his built work: one year of study in art and a graduate course in urban studies. Calatrava went on to earn a doctorate in civil engineering at the Swiss Federal Institute of Technology in Zurich. He met his wife while he was in graduate school—she was studying law—and they made Zurich their home and the base for his principal architecture office.

Trained in the 1960s, Calatrava felt undernourished by the functionalist rhetoric then in vogue in European architecture schools: "It was a time of revolution. To discuss aesthetics was considered bourgeois, decadent." He was frustrated by didactic instruction and wanted to find his own way to understand architecture: "Learning was handed to me.... I preferred to hear a bird singing rather than a person singing like a bird." Dissatisfaction with his architectural education was one reason he went on to study engineering, but his intellectual hunger was stronger. Instead of choosing a major he chose everything. "I love drawing and painting and sculpture. I also love the rigor of mathematics. My decision was to stay in between."

Calatrava spent four years on his doctorate in engineering. His thesis was a systematic examination of foldable—or movable—structures. "Until I was 30, I worked rigorously at this." In that program, Calatrava felt he was unshackled.

To those who think structural engineering is a purely technical field, the idea that it was liberating to Calatrava may seem odd. "Engineering design does not mean calculating things; that is just a small part of it," Calatrava says. For him, engineering supplied the last piece: with it he could solve the entire problem himself. "So finally the architecture design and the engineering design became the same thing."

He has developed a rare knowledge set and it informs all of his design work. The Milwaukee Art Museum addition is such a complete synthesis of design and engineering that it could not have been conceived by someone without training in both fields. This work does not follow Louis Sullivan's most succinct of all architectural axioms relating design to structure, "Form follows function." Structural deductions may be drawn from examining the Milwaukee addition (particularly in section), but the assumption that structure determined the form, or that the form determined the structure, does not follow. Calatrava's priorities are elsewhere and he manipulates structure and form to achieve them. The consistent theme in Calatrava's work is to dramatize and mystify the physics of

Alamillo Bridge and La Cartuja Viaduct, Seville, Spain, 1987–92.

Campo Volantin Footbridge, Bilbao, Spain, 1990–97.

structure. To the observer's eye, his work appears to push stasis to the point of failure, and yet, the structure stands. In resisting collapse it acquires a compelling quality, demanding intellectual examination and aesthetic appreciation of its sculptural form.

The intention is calculated: Calatrava means for his work to be arresting in this way. The engineering techniques he uses to achieve it are not innovative, although his combination of techniques is unique. Here he parts company with Robert Maillart, the pioneering Swiss bridge-builder (1872–1940) whose work has so clearly influenced Calatrava. Maillart, too, was trained as an engineer, and he produced enduring and—like Calatrava—uniquely sculptural architectural work. Unlike Calatrava, however, Maillart was interested in engineering innovation, establishing new principles and using new materials economically. Calatrava is not uninterested in these issues; he employs the principles the great engineers have established, and he prizes them, but engineering invention does not guide his work. Calatrava's work, for example, always employs counterbalance—a technique used by the Romans, so it can hardly be called cutting-edge—but using it, Calatrava achieves some of his most dramatic effects.

There is no problem as challenging as stretching a load-bearing structure across a void, so bridges hold a special place in building history. Calatrava's bridges are what first drew attention to him. There are now more than 30 bridges designed and built by him, almost all of them in Europe. They are characterized by structural bravado and formal innovation. They also betray Calatrava's enduring interest in movement in architecture, which has shown itself in sculptural projects such as the *Shadow Machine* he exhibited in New York and Venice (1992–93) or in buildings such as the Kuwait Pavilion (1991–92) for the World's Fair, Expo '92, in Seville, Spain. Although the bridges do not have moving elements, they are very animated, made so by their curves, the tension in their cables, their asymmetry.

The Alamillo Bridge (1987–92) in Seville, which resembles the Milwaukee Art Museum's bridge but is structurally dissimilar, has a single pylon at one end that leans back at a 58-degree angle. From the pylon, taut cables extend to the deck so the bridge resembles an enormous harp. The brute weight of the cement-filled pylon and the tension in the cables counterbalance the bridge deck. It is beautiful and it works, but it looks illogical, almost frighteningly so, as though the whole assembly should tumble over backwards. Its surprise is in confounding expectations of symmetry. The Alamillo was to have had a mirror-image companion bridge that, sadly, was never built.

In his Campo Volantin pedestrian bridge (1990–97) in Bilbao, Calatrava has curved the glass deck so that it looks as though it is bending with the current of the river over which it flows. There is nothing structurally necessary in that curve—indeed, it requires a support beneath the bridge to compensate for it—but that curve does make the walk across the river a passage, something more likely to be considered as it is experienced by the pedestrian. That expression—more sculptural than structural—is always evident in Calatrava's work. It is as if he is insisting on one's full attention to the experience while his work is occupied.

Calatrava has a large category he calls "links." In this he would gather all his bridges, his Airport Railway Station in Lyon, the BCE Place Gallery and Heritage Square (1987–92) in Toronto, Canada, the Orient Station (1993–98) in Lisbon, Portugal, and the law school faculty library (2004) at the University of Zurich. They are all projects built in found space and each of these creates new connections that stimulate human activity. "The matters that interest me are creating links," he says. "Maybe the most important object or architectural subject of links are bridges, others are stations, others are streets in cities. I like this kind of undefined object. They are not destinations. They are transitional objects. It has the connotation of the place I have not yet been. It has the connotation of discovery."

The Stadelhofen Railway Station (1983–90) in Zurich takes what is potentially the most bleak of urban experiences—the commuter train station—and makes it a fine coherent stop on a journey. The sense of motion is integral to the program and the site, with trains moving through the station and the site wrapping around the base of a hill. Calatrava emphasized it subtly with a series of cut-steel supports for a protective glass canopy. The repeating steel forms angle and recede, following the curve, effortlessly expressing the nature of a transportation node. "What is beautiful in the work of an architect is that we are confronted by the reality of everyday life and as much as we can in this world, we embellish everyday life."

In the BCE Place project, the architect enclosed the voids among buildings on an entire city block with a towering glass-and-steel arcade. Where there had been nothing, restaurants, stores, and cafés sprang up. In Zurich, Calatrava took a vacant lightwell in an older university building and inserted a library, covering it with glass and a brise soleil (mounted inside this time). The entry on a disused side of the building now teems with students coming and going.

BCE Place Gallery and Heritage Square, Toronto, Canada, 1987–92.

Orient Station, Lisbon, Portugal, 1993–98.

Stadelhofen Railway Station, Zurich, Switzerland, 1983–90.

Preliminary sketches of the Milwaukee Art Museum addition, 1996.

THE DESIGN EVOLVES

People say when somebody writes his first novel it is always autobiographical. I think in a way, that this [Milwaukee Art Museum addition] is a little like that—autobiographical—because it has part of my interest in movement and the bridge.

SANTIAGO CALATRAVA, ZURICH, AUGUST 30, 2004

In the Milwaukee Art Museum addition, Calatrava found a problem that could be solved with the things he most liked to design and build, a bridge and a large moving architectural piece. But originally neither the bridge nor the brise soleil was a part of the design.

The first scheme was bold. Calatrava imagined a great hall suspended out past the Lake Michigan shore and hovering above the water. Not only was this idea impractical because of what damage ice and waves could do on a lake more tempestuous than Lake Zurich, but it also placed the building's emphasis on the waterfront, away from the city. Returning to the design, he focused on connecting the museum to the city. The rough outlines of the solution came to him: long galleries running north-south brought the museum's new entry near its southern end in line with one of Milwaukee's principal east-west streets, Wisconsin Avenue. The bridge also became a part of the design, literally connecting the museum's front door with downtown Milwaukee. In July 1995 Calatrava presented this design to the building committee, which embraced it. Work continued on space allocation inside the building.

At the same time, Calatrava had begun to think about the brise soleil. Calatrava had made one rough model that was operated by pulling a string, and he showed it to Bowman and Goldsmith, asking them if he should develop it and present it to the committee. Not wanting to filter any ideas between the architect and the trustees, the two directors said Calatrava should proceed. By February 1996 the architect had a refined model, and a video he could show to the building committee. Immediately, the committee agreed to add the brise soleil. "Everyone loved it," Bowman says. "There was an emotional response to it."

The addition of the brise soleil was brilliant, even necessary, after the museum's new entrance became the terminus to Wisconsin Avenue. When that occurred, the museum acquired a greater urban responsibility and the brise soleil visually raised the building to an appropriately monumental scale that would fill its new role. As one travels east on Wisconsin Avenue, the white wings seem to fill the end of the street and no more persuasion is required to demonstrate the importance of the brise soleil as a gesture to the city.

In March 1996 the design was shown to the public and the fund-raising campaign was launched. The goal was to raise $35 million by the end of the year. Bowman was stunned when that target was exceeded. The late Jane Bradley Pettit gave the museum its largest donation—$13 million—on the condition that the museum never bear an individual's name in place of the city's. Harry and Betty Quadracci gave another $10 million.

The success of the campaign demonstrated the community's enthusiasm for the project. Thinking that they could afford to expand the campaign, the trustees raised the goal to $50 million and added features to the building they had rejected earlier for cost reasons. Parking would go underground, beneath the museum, instead of forming a miserable concrete forecourt to the new building. To gain more meeting rooms, the south end of the building was extended. Later, a brilliant landscaping program would be added. What became known as the Cudahy Gardens was the last project designed by and completed under the supervision of the great landscape architect Dan Kiley, who died in February 2004 at age 91.

Calatrava had resolved the design of the long gallery in the meantime. An early idea had the gallery sheltered by a steeply angled roof that extended nearly to the ground along the west side. Calatrava had imagined the form as being like a great wave breaking on the lakeshore. The trouble was, once again, the problematic relationship created between the city and the museum if the west side of the building, the side facing the city, were made to appear closed-off and opaque. Calatrava realized this would be a mistake and thus opened both the east and west gallery to the light.

Some of the ideas and forms that emerged in this stage of the design are related to a visit Calatrava made to Frank Lloyd Wright's Johnson Wax Building (1936–39) in Racine, Wisconsin. Echoes of that building are evident in the rounded corners and the striation, or reveals, that relieves the massive walls of the museum. The architect developed his cunning solution to the transition from the lower-level parking garage to the great hall after looking at Wright's work. A hole in the floor of Calatrava's large reception hall gives a view of an open drum with stairs descending around either side, leading down to the parking level. The drum serves as a transition between the symmetry of the great hall and the off-axis garage entry. This is similar to the way in which Wright used rounded forms to identify zones and create transition spaces.

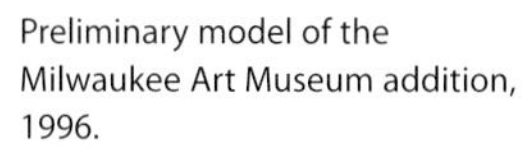

Preliminary model of the Milwaukee Art Museum addition, 1996.

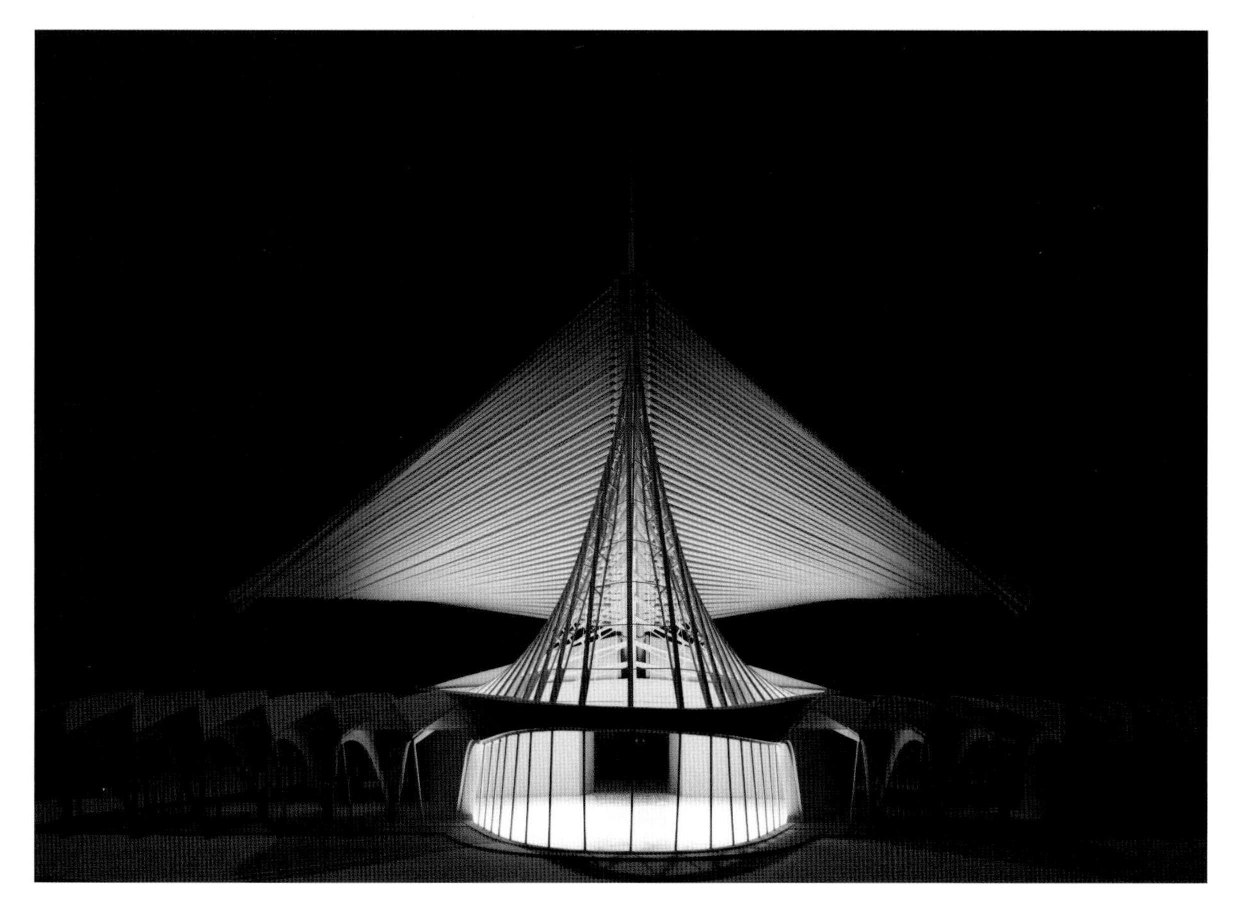

Concrete arches take shape along the east side of the pavilion.

The arches of the special exhibition gallery keep this space free of internal supports.

An aerial view shows the building taking final shape.

A dense thicket of reinforcing steel ensures the stability of the Quadracci Pavilion's main floor.

FOLLOWING PAGES
The Schroeder Galleria runs the length of the Milwaukee Art Museum addition along the west side.

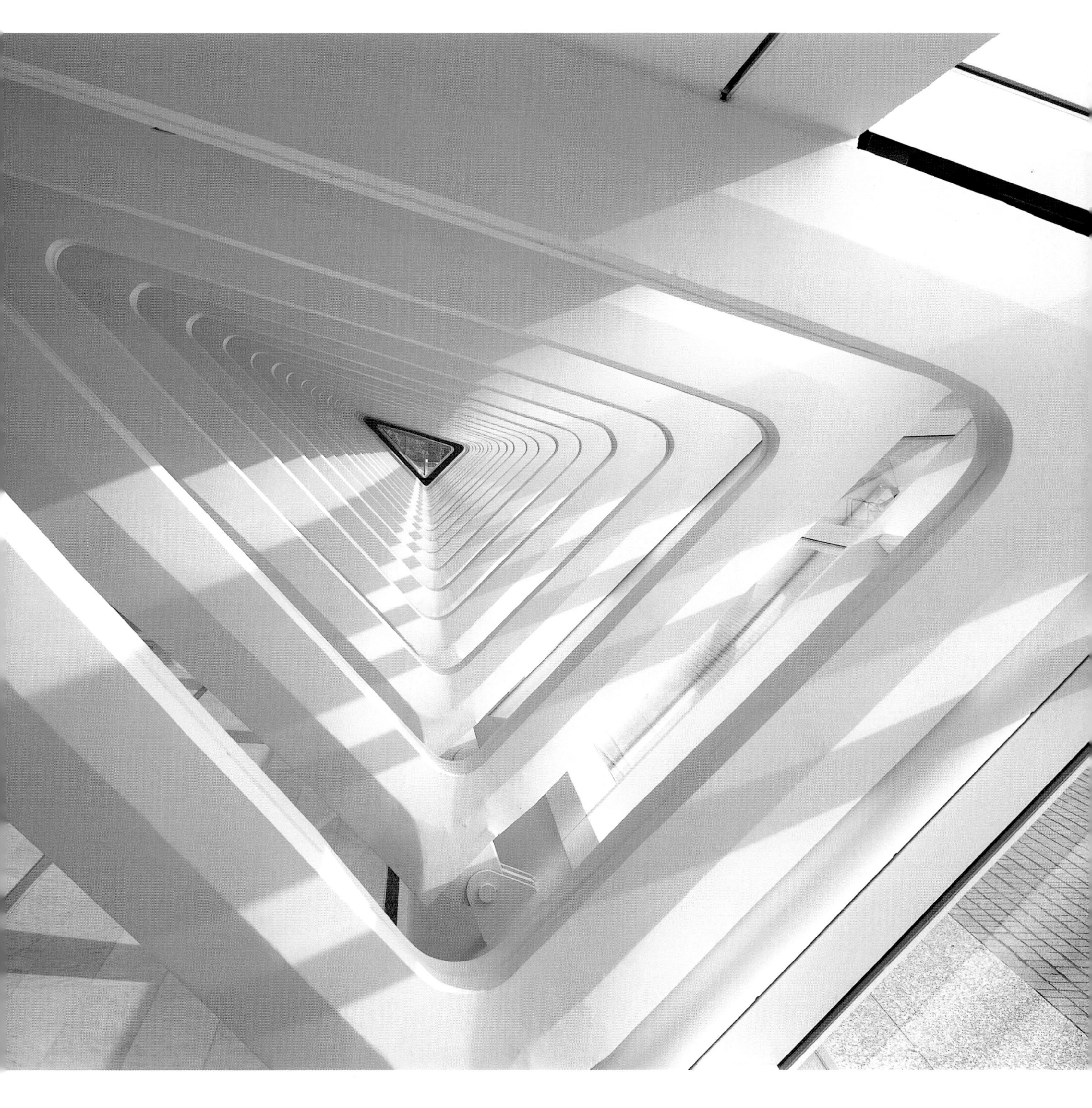

View, looking southeast, from inside Windhover Hall.

The Baumgartner Galleria,
on the east side of the building,
features works from the museum's
permanent collection.

Two views of the east end of the pavilion, showing the cantilevered prow of the "ring beam."

BUILDING IT

Many years ago construction was the guild spirit. All these people working together like brothers. I believe in some buildings you can feel this; you gain links to people that go beyond. It's like choosing your family.

SANTIAGO CALATRAVA, ZURICH, AUGUST 30, 2004

The museum, Kahler, and all of us were on a mission. There was no way it wasn't going to happen.

STEVE CHAMBERLIN, MILWAUKEE, SEPTEMBER 8, 2004

The first thing executive director Christopher Goldsmith told the eighteen construction firms from across the United States competing to build the Milwaukee Art Museum addition was to put their checkbooks away. He said anyone who called a museum board member would be disqualified. It wasn't about politics or connections, he said. It was about getting the most qualified firm. In the end, Milwaukee-based C. G. Schmidt won the job.

Steve Chamberlin, president of Schmidt, first saw the building as an operable model: "I looked at it and thought, this is amazing." His job would be to figure out how to construct it, to hire all the subcontractors who would build it, and to schedule the job so no time would be wasted and materials would be on hand as they were needed—no sooner, no later. Among other things, he would have to find subcontractors to make building components that had never been made before or tested before in a society that seems to love nothing more than a lawsuit. Who exactly would fabricate the blades for the wings and create the mechanics to lift them?

A conventional building is composed of columns and beams on a grid, and the object with such a building is to get it built for as little as possible. Here, the structural system fit no formula. "Everything was custom for this job," says John Kissinger, the lead structural engineer with Graef, Anhalt, Schloemer & Associates of Milwaukee, the engineering firm selected for the project.

Among other things, the unconventional nature of the building made it impossible to do more than guess the costs. Estimates made by a firm that had built Calatrava's work before proved to be just as wrong as everybody else's. In an unusual arrangement for the construction industry, the team was paid on a cost-plus basis.

View, looking east, inside Windhover Hall.

View of Lake Michigan from the prow of Windhover Hall.

View from the lakefront of the cantilevered prow.

In the fall of 1996 a group composed of Kissinger, Kahler, and Chamberlin, along with representatives from two other firms that would later be dropped from the project, made a trip to Europe to spend ten days with Calatrava and to look at some of his built work. They traveled to Zurich, they went to Valencia, Paris, and Lyon. They spent time at his home with his family, they went out to dinner, and one night they all went to the opera together. Chamberlin says, "He [Calatrava] was trying to find the right people. It was not just about cost and schedule. I took off my builder's hat and said, 'They have a special mission here.'" Over the course of that visit the team from Milwaukee came to understand what level of finish Calatrava expected and the core team developed a loyalty to the architect.

Kahler's firm had nearly one-third of his firm's staff and, he says, twenty-five percent of its computer capacity dedicated to the Milwaukee Art Museum addition for the seven-year duration of the project. For his part, Kahler spent time on the museum project that some colleagues thought he should be using to get new projects. "I wanted to do it right for the institution and the community." For Kahler, who would retire from his architecture firm to start a solo practice not long after the addition was completed, the Calatrava project was a chance to stretch as he had not since the addition to the Saarinen structure: "All the skills I had went into this."

There are three elements in this building, any one of which alone would have made it an architectural and structural marvel: the brise soleil, the pedestrian bridge, and the pavilion, now named Windhover Hall—a column-free oval-shaped space 293 feet long with a glass roof rising up 90 feet, and a 90-foot glass-encased cantilevered "prow" that draws visitors inexorably with its sensational view of Lake Michigan. That there is a 50-foot cantilever on the south side of the building seems scarcely worth mentioning in the company of the other structural extravagances, even though it would be a scene-stealer in a lesser building.

A descriptive nomenclature sprang up among those working on the project to identify pieces in the building: they named certain parts the "wishbone," the "fishbone," the "hammerhead," and the "boomerangs." But it was the "ring beam"—the least showy piece of all in the end—that was the most difficult to engineer and build. The ring beam encircles the pavilion at the ceiling, and it forms the long cantilever at the east end, or prow. It carries the weight of the huge roof—the brise soleil, the glass ceiling, its framing, and the mast—and transfers that load to the ground through four large piers. The ring is embedded with 100 steel cables—50 running through each side and tied at the west end of the hall—to maximize the strength of the beam. "When we started removing the formwork and pulled the scaffolding away, we couldn't believe [the cantilever] would stay up. It's just hanging out there," Chamberlin said. It did hold, of course, and its daring is evident in the construction photographs where it plainly looks like the trapeze act it really is.

The café is located under the east end of the reception hall and is wrapped with the same wall of glass.

OPPOSITE
View of the glass wall of the pavilion.

View of the Quadracci Pavilion and Burke Brise Soleil, looking south from the sculpture garden with Alexander Liberman's *Argo* (1974).

usbank

View, looking north, of the Quadracci Pavilion and Burke Brise Soleil.

Eero Saarinen, TWA Terminal, John F. Kennedy Airport, New York, 1962. Ezra Stoller © Esto.

Fully constructed, the prow is encased in two stories of floor-to-ceiling glass, one at the pavilion level and another at the café one floor below. With the inevitable movement in such a long cantilever, and Calatrava's requirement for large pieces of angled curving glass, the engineer had another problem. "The question for the engineer to determine was how much movement there would be and detail the glass and [its] framing to accommodate that without fracturing the glass," Kissinger said. The calculations were exceptionally difficult, but then finding someone to make the glass was harder. No one wanted to be responsible if it did not work. Finally, a manufacturer in Spain was found to make the two toughest panels in the center; the rest were done by a Wisconsin company.

From the exterior, the glass wall that angles to the ground blunts the raw drama of the cantilever. Something else emerges in its stead, though; in the profile of the glass-encased prow is the unmistakable echo of Eero Saarinen's own birdlike building, the TWA Terminal. This is Calatrava's homage to the man who built the original structure for the Milwaukee Art Center.

Like Calatrava's other bridges, the one he designed for the Milwaukee Art Museum addition is arresting to look at and appears to defy structural logic. The bridge spans four lanes of traffic and ascends roughly two stories from the museum to reach the downtown business district just opposite. Nine thin cables extend from a mast to the deck and twice that number from the back of the mast to the ring beam. While the cables help stabilize and support the bridge, it is the 192-foot-long pylon—angled at 48 degrees—that does most of the work, counterbalancing the 231-foot-long deck of the bridge. Counterbalancing permitted, even encouraged, the elegant thinness of the bridge's profile. This engineering method requires minimal structure; lightness is a virtue. The weight of the entire 175-ton bridge is transferred to the ground through two structural supports, dubbed boomerangs—each weighing 40,000 pounds—flanking the bridge where it passes beneath the mast.

To assemble the bridge deck, 24-foot-long hollow steel sections, or box girders, were hoisted onto scaffolding and—to make certain the tension in the cables would be right—loaded with concrete blocks equaling the weight of the granite that would later pave the bridge. Only then could the sections be welded into place. With the exception of the cables, which were made by Bridon International of Doncaster, England, every piece of the bridge was fabricated in Menomonee Falls, Wisconsin, by Duwe Metal Products, Inc., a shop that had never done anything this unconventional or big before, and welcomed the challenge. All told, it took 32,000 hours to fabricate and build the bridge.

While welding continues on what workmen called the "boomerangs," a section of the bridge is lowered into place.

Over fifty steel cables run through each side of the ring beam and are tied at the west end, at the base of the pylon.

The pylon is set at the junction between the pedestrian bridge and the pavilion.

OPPOSITE
View of the entrance to the Quadracci Pavilion.

FOLLOWING PAGES
View, looking west toward the bridge, of the base of the pylon, called the "hammerhead" by those on the job.

Nine cables run from the pylon to the bridge, and eighteen from the pylon back to the pavilion.

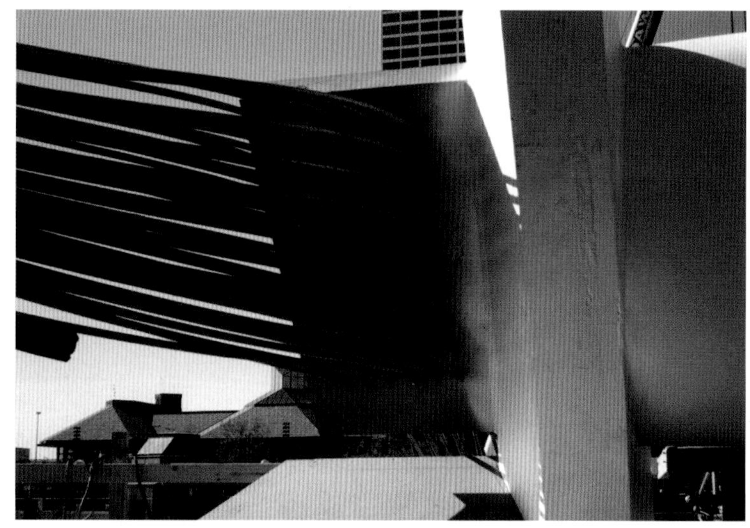

usbank
Northwestern Mutual

Two views, looking west and south, of the entrance to the Quadracci Pavilion from the Reiman Pedestrian Bridge.

View of the pylon from beneath the stairs at the east end of the bridge.

FOLLOWING PAGES
View, looking east, of the Reiman Pedestrian Bridge, Quadracci Pavilion, and Burke Brise Soleil.

MILWAUKEE
ART MUSEUM

The long, north-south expanse of Calatrava's addition to the original museum complex contains two gallerias alongside a core space—containing the museum's shop, its auditorium, and a special-exhibition gallery—that is formed of a succession of independent, supporting classical arches. Arches are more efficient for wide spans than the post-and-beam structure usually used now. But, being more complex to engineer, arches are rarely used. "Counterbalance is a lost art and Calatrava is reviving that," Kissinger says. Throughout the galleries, the precise repetition and alignment of the arches was critical to Calatrava's intentions. If one curve was out of line, the effect would be destroyed.

Calatrava is emphatic about treating all spaces in his buildings as significant. So, garages, which often serve as entry and introduction to buildings for drivers, receive the same level of design attention from him as any other area. The Milwaukee Art Museum's underground garage may be the most splendid in America with great repetitive arch supports similar to those in the gallery above.

"One pour and that's it," says Chamberlin. Compound curves shape virtually every arch and surface in the addition, making the concrete work just about as intricate to accomplish as a mosaic. C. G. Schmidt tried to find a subcontractor who could build the wood forms into which the concrete would be poured, but after the prototypes by two companies did not come up to the required standards, Chamberlin realized it would have to be done by his crew on-site. The basement became a workshop for building plywood forms. "It looked like an auto body shop down there," Chamberlin said. They used the technique that would yield the best results, cutting solid pieces of wood to form every surface, instead of the cheaper method of using wooden slats to piece together forms that inevitably produced roughness and seams in the concrete surface. Some of Calatrava's European work—including the Stadelhofen Railway Station in Zurich—had been constructed with the cheaper method and Chamberlin had been surprised at the crudeness of the work. In Milwaukee, the concrete would have to be as near to flawless as he could get it.

Making wood forms is like constructing a building inside out. The object is to perfectly shape the cavity the concrete will fill by constructing a plywood frame for the void. The plywood was laser-cut and then steamed in order to achieve the correct curves. In addition, every gap in each form was filled in. Lastly, the forms were lined with an epoxylike substance to prevent the concrete from picking up the grain of the plywood. Such forms, which are typically used a dozen times or more on a conventional project, could be used no more than three times here before they had to be replaced, and, in between uses, each imperfection had to be patched and the inside recoated. Some, like the $50,000 form specially crafted for the café ceiling—this was the one known by those on the job as the fishbone—were used only once. Chamberlin found a workman on his knees, filing by hand the radius of a compound curve on a form in preparation for pouring the concrete piers. "This was really a craftsman project," Kissinger said.

Fifteen pairs of supports spring from the central spine of the museum's underground garage.

OPPOSITE
View, looking south, down the length of the Baumgartner Galleria, along the east side of the museum.

One pair of concrete supports was so complicated they could not be drawn. These support the south cantilever and angle off in three different directions from their bases. A model of the columns was made in clay, shown to Calatrava, and kept on site where the builders could and did refer to it as they needed.

Engineers also made models at one-quarter scale to demonstrate concepts. They created one model of the boomerang just to show how it would work. "There's something about the physical thing that convinces people," Kissinger says. As it turned out, these same scale models helped convince people to give money to fund-raisers for the project.

Depending on performance requirements, steel reinforcement bars are placed inside forms before the concrete is poured. Chamberlin says, "There's so much reinforcing steel it is basically a steel building covered with concrete." Laying in some 2,100 tons of steel bars in this building, the contractors worried that in some areas where the reinforcing was especially dense the concrete could not get through it to distribute evenly throughout the form.

Kahler had to design details in a way that would be compatible with Calatrava's scheme. Kahler was trained as a modernist and he was an admirer of Louis Kahn, who advised him on his master's thesis at Princeton, so this work was for him a kind of ego-sublimation rarely witnessed in a profession not known for its modesty. Kahler redesigned the fixtures that fit into the gallery lightwells, reworking Calatrava's design to make it more compatible with the building's organic, soft lines. Calatrava agreed that they were better and they were built. In his office, Kahler kept watch over his staff: "They were used to using stuff from the hardware store; they were not used to working with expensive materials and a large budget."

Calatrava continued his monthly trips to Milwaukee during construction. "He doesn't swoop in, do his color renderings and swoop out," says Chamberlin. The architect ate pizza with the contractors in the construction trailer on the site. When he was asked by the trustees or the directors, he attended fund-raisers. In a way, the job assumed the character of a 13th-century Gothic cathedral under construction, not that it lasted for generations, but that significant modifications and decisions were being made cooperatively as construction proceeded. The architect counseled the contractors continually against making anything more difficult than it had to be, and quietly Calatrava expressed his complete faith in their ability to do the job beautifully. In the end, the people who worked on the job thanked him for asking so much of them.

This multiple structural junction was so difficult to draw that it was modeled in clay for ease of understanding.

Ironworkers position a steel reinforcing cage before a form is completed.

Custom forms were constructed throughout the building to give the concrete walls their seamless reveals.

OPPOSITE
Alexander Calder's 1973 mobile *Red, Black and Blue* turns above the entrance to the pavilion from the garage beneath.

THE LAST CHALLENGE

By February 2001 the building was nearing completion; the formal opening was scheduled for October 10. With just eight months to go, it was suddenly clear that the plan for the brise soleil was not working. Because it is exceptionally light, durable, and would not require repainting, a carbon-fiber material had been proposed for the tubes that would form the wings. But there had been difficulties finding anyone who could handle the material and fabricate the tubes. There were reports that a factory would have to be reconfigured just to get the job done and the price for the carbon fiber was very high. On top of that, the engineer wanted to run a wind-tunnel test simulating the conditions the carbon fiber would have to withstand. That test alone would cost another $1 million. Already the building had exceeded several projected budgets, and knowing that they were over budget, it would have been easy for the museum's trustees to abandon this last piece of the building for cost reasons; but they did not consider backing down.

View of the Quadracci Pavilion in the summer of 2001 prior to the installation of the fins of the brise soleil.

It fell to Calatrava to find a solution. The carbon fiber was abandoned and he decided to use steel, as he had suggested earlier. But the ring beam that would take the weight of the brise soleil was built to carry carbon fiber, not steel. Calatrava went to a very thin gauge of steel: one-quarter inch or less was what he wanted, and he needed a contractor who could do such precise work. There are 72 individual blades, 36 on each side, ranging in length from 26 to 105 feet. Few steel fabricators have the machines that will allow them to work with steel that thin, so Calatrava searched for a while before one was found in Spain that met the requirements. Another compromise was necessary: the carbon-fiber wings were to have stayed open in winds up to 40 miles per hour. When the material was changed, the wings could be open in winds of up to 23 miles per hour, closing automatically when the winds picked up speed. By the end of March, Calatrava was able to tell the museum board how much it would cost to produce the wings and get its approval. In his office, detailed planning began. In early June—with just four months until the museum opening—a tolerance test to make sure the thin steel would work was run and fabrication began in Spain. Calatrava himself supervised the production and approved the quality.

The C. G. Schmidt office, which would manage the installation of the wings on the building, faced other hurdles in establishing a schedule. Normally, pieces as large as these steel wings would be sent by ship, but that would take months and the opening would be missed. There was little choice but to pay to have the pieces flown to Milwaukee. Two of the world's largest transport planes—Russian-built Antonov 124 cargo haulers that were sold after the country's collapse—were leased from Lufthansa to get the wings to Milwaukee. There was so little time that the fabricator had not been able to finish painting all of them; that would be completed in Milwaukee.

With work on the exterior largely completed, the building awaited the arrival of the steel fins that would form the wings of the brise soleil.

In a final month of feverish activity
before the museum's opening,
the rotating shafts and steel fins
were attached to the spine of the
brise soleil.

The steel fins for the brise soleil were nested in the belly of the plane like wine bottles in a rack and flown directly to Milwaukee. The pieces were shuttled from General Mitchell International Airport to the museum on eighteen-wheel trucks in the middle of the night when streets could be closed to traffic most easily. The bundles of fins were so long that they had to be lifted by crane from the bed of one truck to another truck waiting around the corner whenever a turn had to be made. They were installed just in time for the opening.

The addition cost $100 million, with a further cost of $20 million for the Cudahy Gardens, reorganization of the permanent collection, and interest and development costs. Russell Bowman was asked often about spending the money on a museum addition instead of art, and he had a ready reply: "I could have bought one Picasso, but I could not have transformed people's perception of the institution." After the opening the museum's attendance increased dramatically. To potential art donors the building promises that a committed institution with a future is prepared to care for their gift. Soon after the addition was built, the museum received Marcia and Granvil Specks' German Expressionist prints, an internationally esteemed collection given by a Chicago couple.

FOLLOWING PAGES
Views of the entire addition to the Milwaukee Art Museum, including the Cudahy Gardens designed by Dan Kiley.

When Calatrava is asked why movement should be a part of architecture, his answer is almost Miesian: "Because it is possible, and because it is possible it is part of our time." He is criticized by some for the lavish expressiveness of his work, by others for an impure approach to engineering. But such criticisms seem pointless when the architect would willingly agree that his work is expressive and his engineering unorthodox. He does not expect or care for his work to be evaluated on those terms. He does not pretend to be the standard-bearer for a new architectural style—style is just the invention of critics who need classifications, he says—nor does he make a strenuous argument for functionality. (Truth be told, the brise soleil does not do a wonderful job of keeping sunlight out.) But Calatrava will make a passionate case for art and for beauty and for the right of ordinary people to enjoy them. "Architecture can really touch people. You discover that architecture is not something functional, that people embrace architecture as they embrace painting or as they embrace sculpture." That's what he wants ultimately, to bring some beauty into life and make people feel it.

Milwaukee wanted a striking building and the city got it. The addition called for supreme efforts from everyone involved, fund-raisers to concrete-form makers, and they performed at a level that astonished themselves. In some of the construction photographs, the building looks like a great big dinosaur that could throw men off its back at any moment. This impression comes partly from Calatrava's zoomorphic forms, but it is also just the plain truth. People pressed hard against the tolerance levels of materials, knowledge, and ability to make this building. So, in addition to the building, Milwaukee got to find out that it was capable of doing amazing things.

THE CUDAHY
GARDENS

MILWAUKEE
ART MUSEUM

LEFT
TURN
LANE

Magnetic
North
NO
PARKING
ANY
TIME

usbank
usbank

Interior view of the museum store, with display cases designed by Santiago Calatrava.

Interior view of the Lubar Auditorium at the north end of the Quadracci Pavilion.

OPPOSITE
Interior view of the entrance elevator in Windhover Hall.

EXIT
EXIT

Project Personnel: Milwaukee Art Museum, Quadracci Pavilion

Architect Selection Committee

Allen L. Samson, Chair
Donald Baumgartner
Roger L. Boerner
Marilyn Bradley
Margaret Chester
John Morris Dixon
Dudley J. Godfrey, Jr.
Robert Greenstreet
Susan M. Jennings
A. Raymond Kehm
Raymond R. Krueger
Marianne Lubar
Wayne R. Lueders
P. Michael Mahoney
Richard R. Pieper
Betty Quadracci
Harry V. Quadracci
Suzanne Selig
David Uihlein, Jr.
Frederick Vogel III
Hope Melamed Winter

Building Committee

Donald Baumgartner, Chair
Raymond R. Krueger
P. Michael Mahoney
Frank J. Pelisek
Harry V. Quadracci
Mary Ladish Selander
David Uihlein, Jr.
Robert A. Wagner

Russell Bowman
Christopher Goldsmith

Architect

Santiago Calatrava, S.A.
Parkring 11
8002 Zurich, Switzerland
Santiago Calatrava DESIGN ARCHITECT

Architect of Record

Kahler Slater Architects
111 West Wisconsin Avenue
Milwaukee, WI 53203-2501

David Kahler, FAIA PRINCIPAL IN CHARGE
Lou Stippich, AIA PROJECT MANAGER
Erv Schloemer, AIA SENIOR PROJECT ARCHITECT
Roger Retzlaff, AIA PROJECT ARCHITECT

Interior Designer

Kahler Slater Architects

Cudahy Gardens Landscape Architect

Dan Kiley
Office of Dan Kiley
East Farm
Charlotte, VT 05445

Engineers

STRUCTURAL AND CIVIL
Graef, Anhalt, Schloemer & Associates
One Honey Creek Corporate Center
125 South 84th Street, Suite 401
Milwaukee, WI 53214–1470

MECHANICAL AND ELECTRICAL
Ring & DuChateau, Inc.
10101 Innovation Drive, Suite 200
Milwaukee, WI 53226

General Contractor

C. G. Schmidt, Inc.
11777 West Lake Park Drive
Milwaukee, WI 53224

Building Excavation

Schneider Excavating, Inc.
20079 West Main Street
Lannon, WI 53046

Edward E. Gillen Co.
218 West Becher Street
Milwaukee, WI 53207

Consultants

LIGHTING
George Sexton Associates
2121 Wisconsin Avenue NW, Suite 220
Washington, DC 20007

Structural System Formwork

Patent Construction Systems
135 East Pittsburgh Avenue
Milwaukee, WI 53204

Peri GmbH
89259 Weissenhorn
Germany

Reiman Pedestrian Bridge

FABRICATION
Duwe Metal Products, Inc.
N57 W13500 Carman Avenue
Menomonee Falls, WI 53051

ERECTION
C. D. Smith Construction
889 E. Johnson Street
Fond du Lac, WI 54936-1006

LOCKED-COIL CABLES
Bridon International
Doncaster, England

Burke Brise Soleil

MECHANICAL EQUIPMENT DESIGNER
Neenah Engineering, Inc.
2416 Industrial Drive
Neenah, WI 54956

OPERATING CONTROLS AND HYDRAULICS
The Oilgear Company
2300 South 51st Street
Milwaukee, WI 53219–2340

MECHANICAL OPERATING EQUIPMENT
Lunda Construction Company
620 Gebhardt Road
Black River Falls, WI 54615

METAL FINS
Ingemetal, S.A.
Paseo Rosales no. 26, office 11
50008 Zaragoza, Spain

Curtainwall and Skylights

INSTALLATION
Super Sky Products, Inc.
10301 North Enterprise Drive
Mequon, WI 53092

GLASS
Viracon, Inc.
800 Park Drive
Owatonna, MN 55060

Cricursa, S.A.
Pol. Ind. Coll de la Manya
08400 Granollers
Barcelona, Spain

SKYLIGHT FABRICATION
Columbia Wire & Iron Works, Inc.
5555 North Channell Avenue
Portland, OR 97217

Metal Roofing

Overly Manufacturing Company
574 West Otterman Street
Greensburg, PA 15601-0070

Architectural Materials

INSTALLATION
Heuler Tile Company
N16 W23250 Stoneridge Drive
Waukesha, WI 53188

Bill Dentinger Masonry
N29 W2275 Marjean Lane
Waukesha, WI 53186

UNDERLAYMENT
Acoustical Floors of Wisconsin
675 Industrial Court, Suite C
Hartland, WI 53029

CONCRETE
Central Ready Mixed, L.P.
5013 West State Street
Milwaukee, WI 53208

REINFORCING STEEL
Ambassador Steel
W229 N2520 Duplainville Road
Waukesha, WI 53186

GRANITE
Cold Spring Granite, Inc.
202 3rd Avenue South
Cold Spring, MN 56320

MARBLE
SICEA Marmi SRL
Via Aurelia, 27
55045 Pietrasanta, Italy

WOOD FLOORING
Aacer Flooring, LLC
970 Ogden Road
Peshtigo, WI 54157

Entrance Elevator

Kone, Inc.
3225 Gateway Road, Suite 500
Brookfield, WI 53045

Plumbing

Grunau Company, Inc.
1100 West Anderson Road
Oak Creek, WI 53154

Electrical Installation

Pieper Electric, Inc.
5070 North 35th Street
Milwaukee, WI 53209

HVAC System

Wenninger Mechanical Services
16875 West Ryerson Road
New Berlin, WI 53151

Building Control Systems

Johnson Controls, Inc.
5757 North Green Bay Avenue
Milwaukee, WI 53209

Drywall Contractor

Olympic Wall Systems, Inc.
17150 West Pheasant Drive
Milwaukee, WI 53005

Painting

Porta-Painting, Inc.
608 South Street
Milwaukee, WI 53204

Water Feature Architect

Dan Euser Water Architecture
Richmond Hill, Ontario, Canada

Landscaping

Stano Landscaping, Inc.
6565 North Industrial Road
Milwaukee, WI 53223

Interior views of the Quadracci Suite in the South Wing.

OPPOSITE
Site plan.

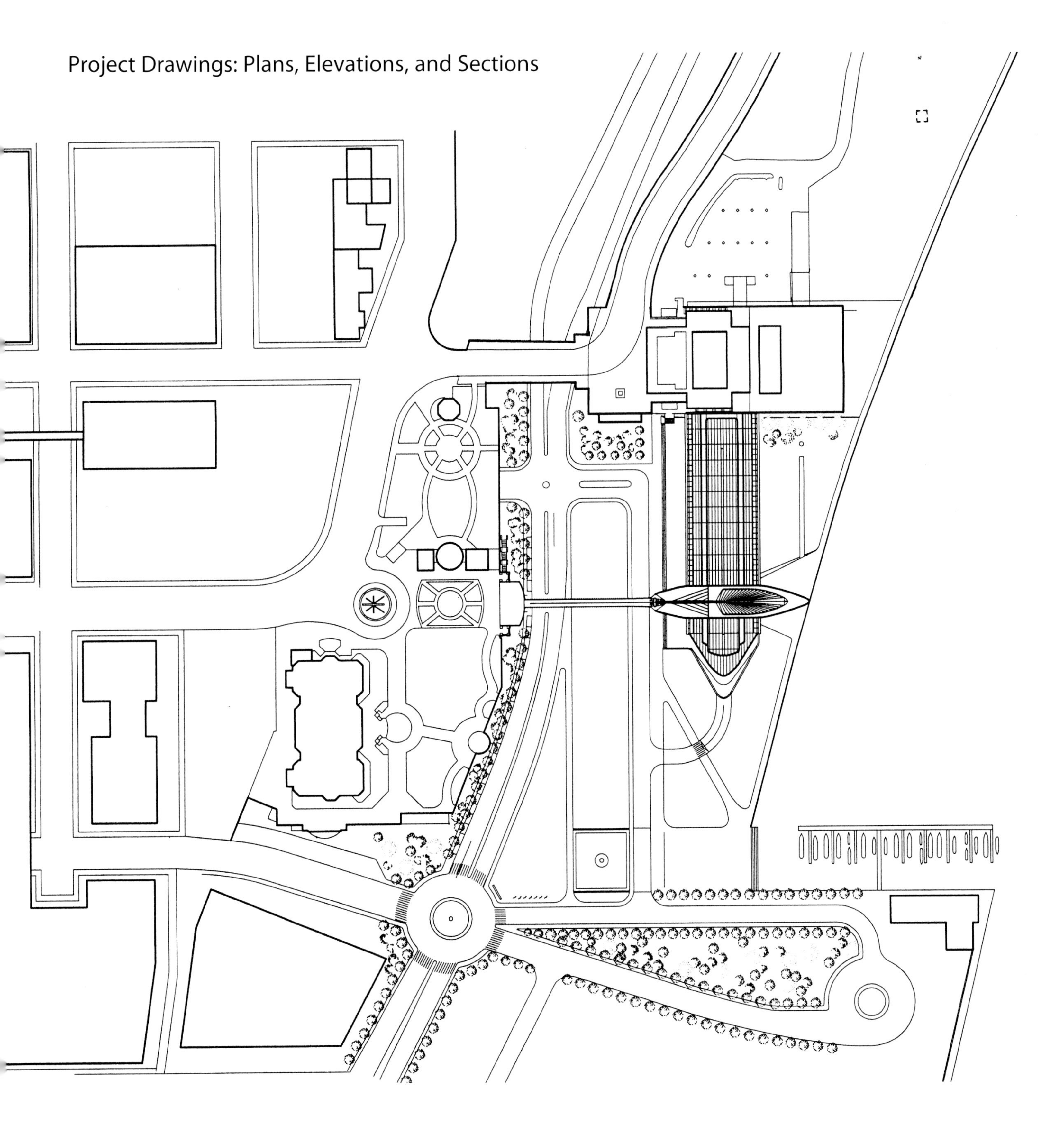

South elevation.

Cross section.

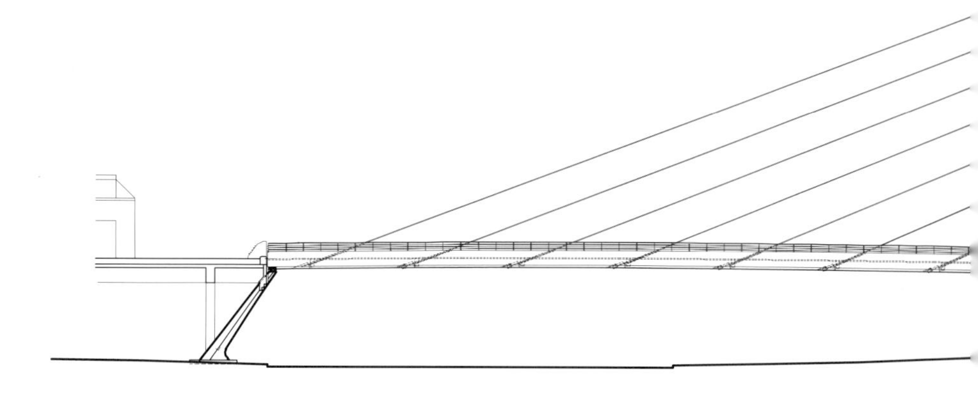

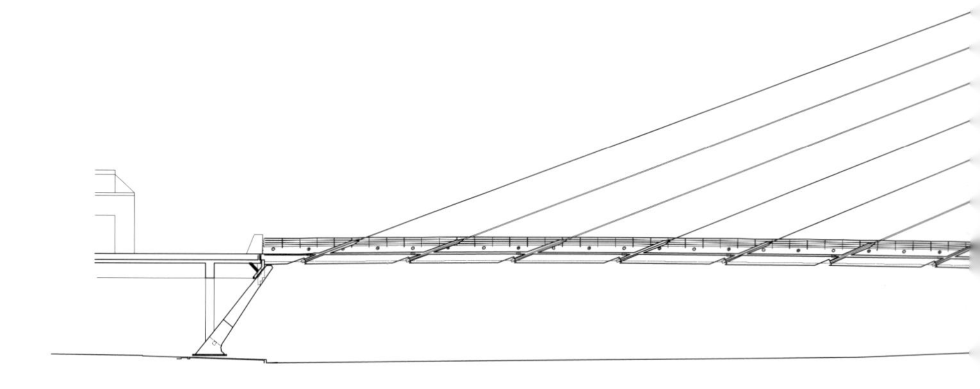

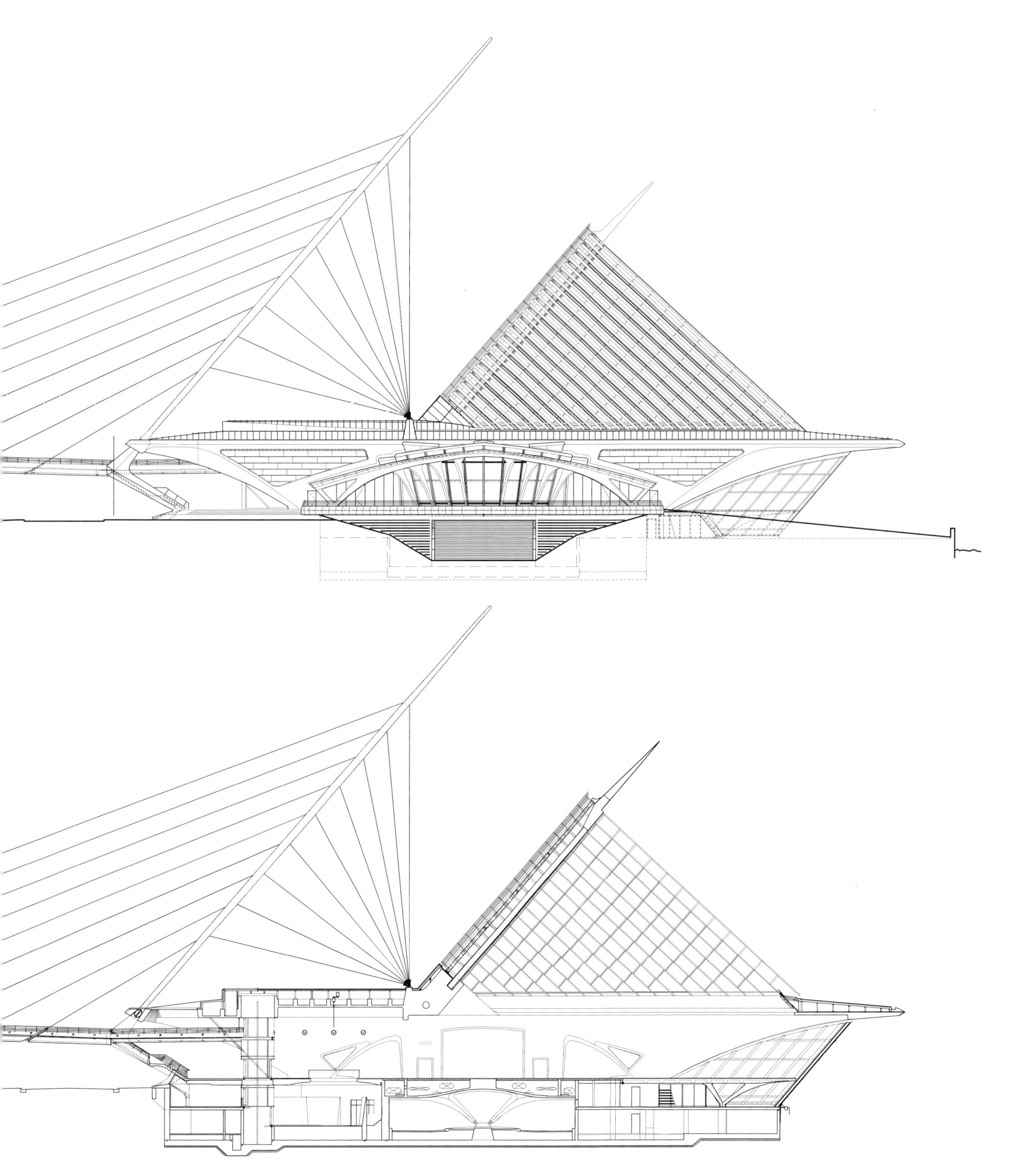

Longitudinal section.

East elevation.

West elevation.

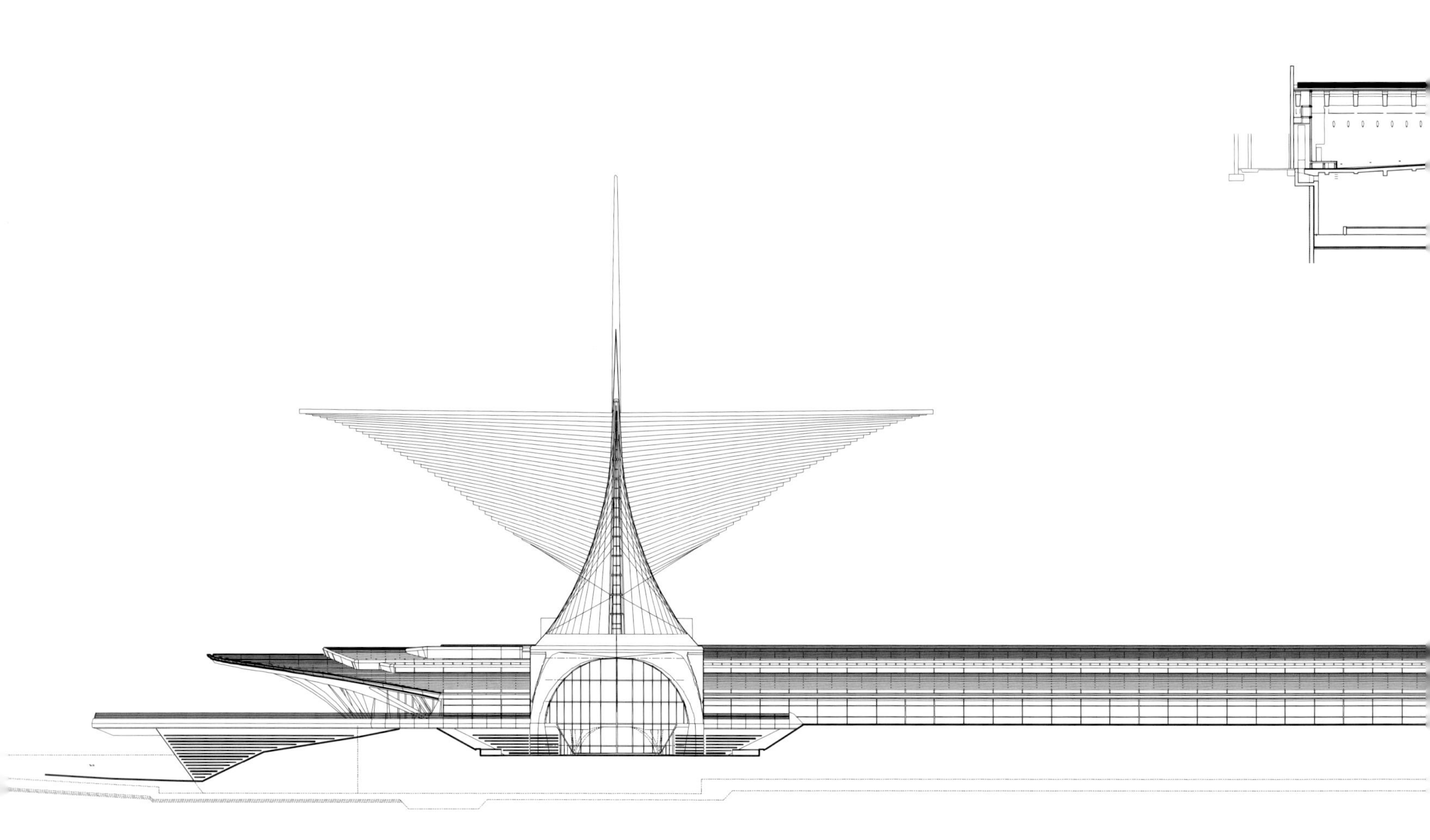

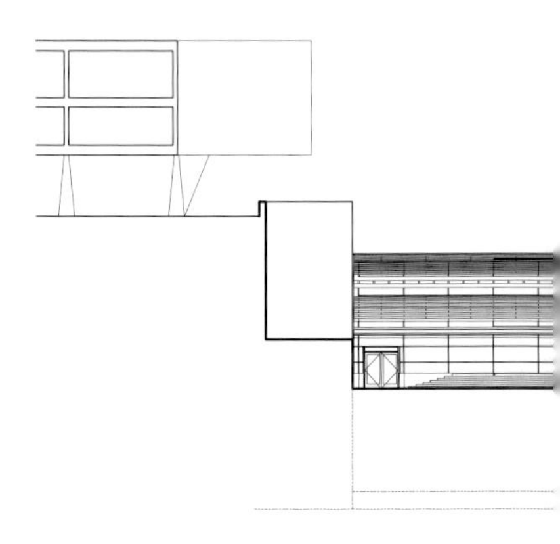

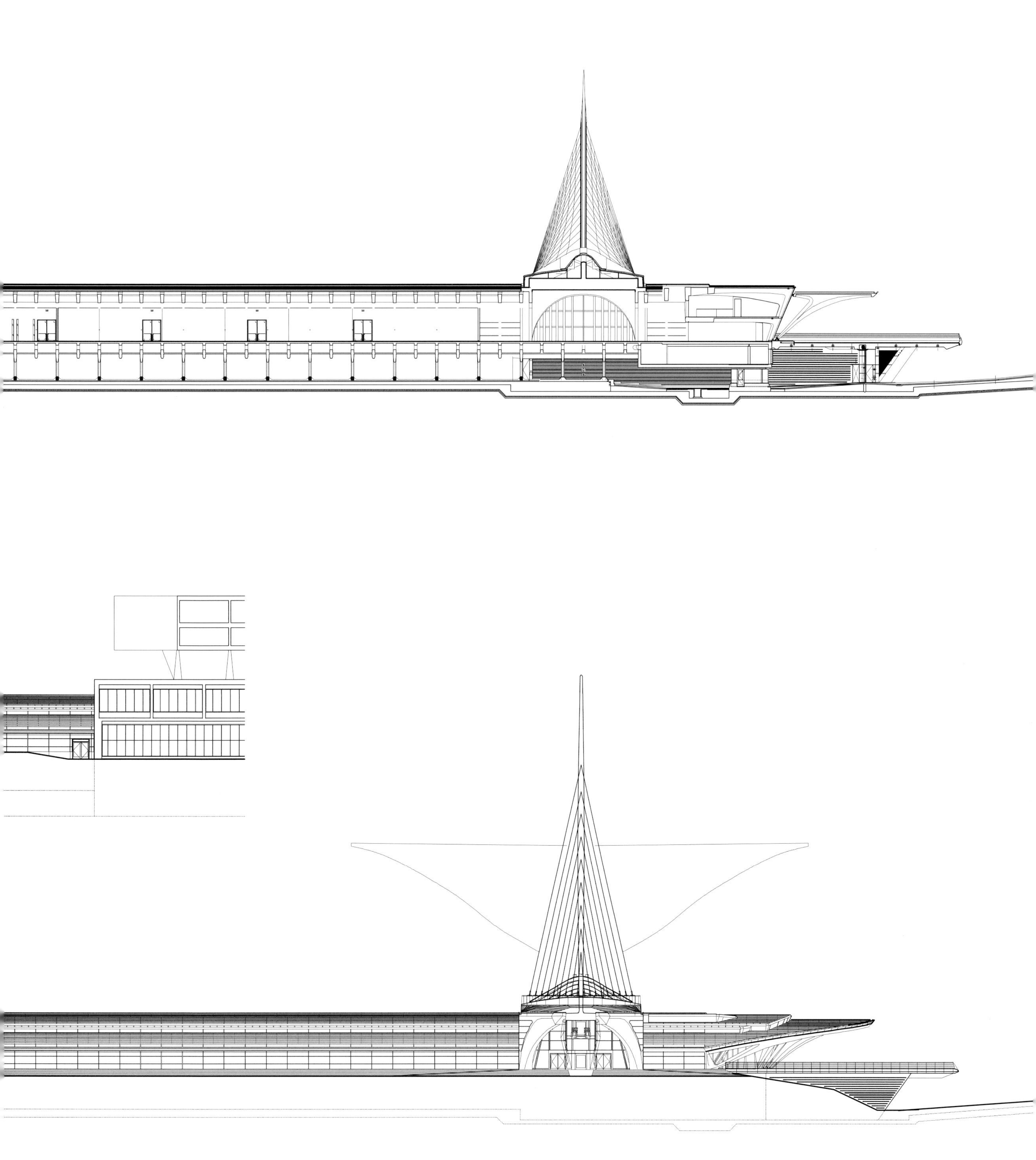

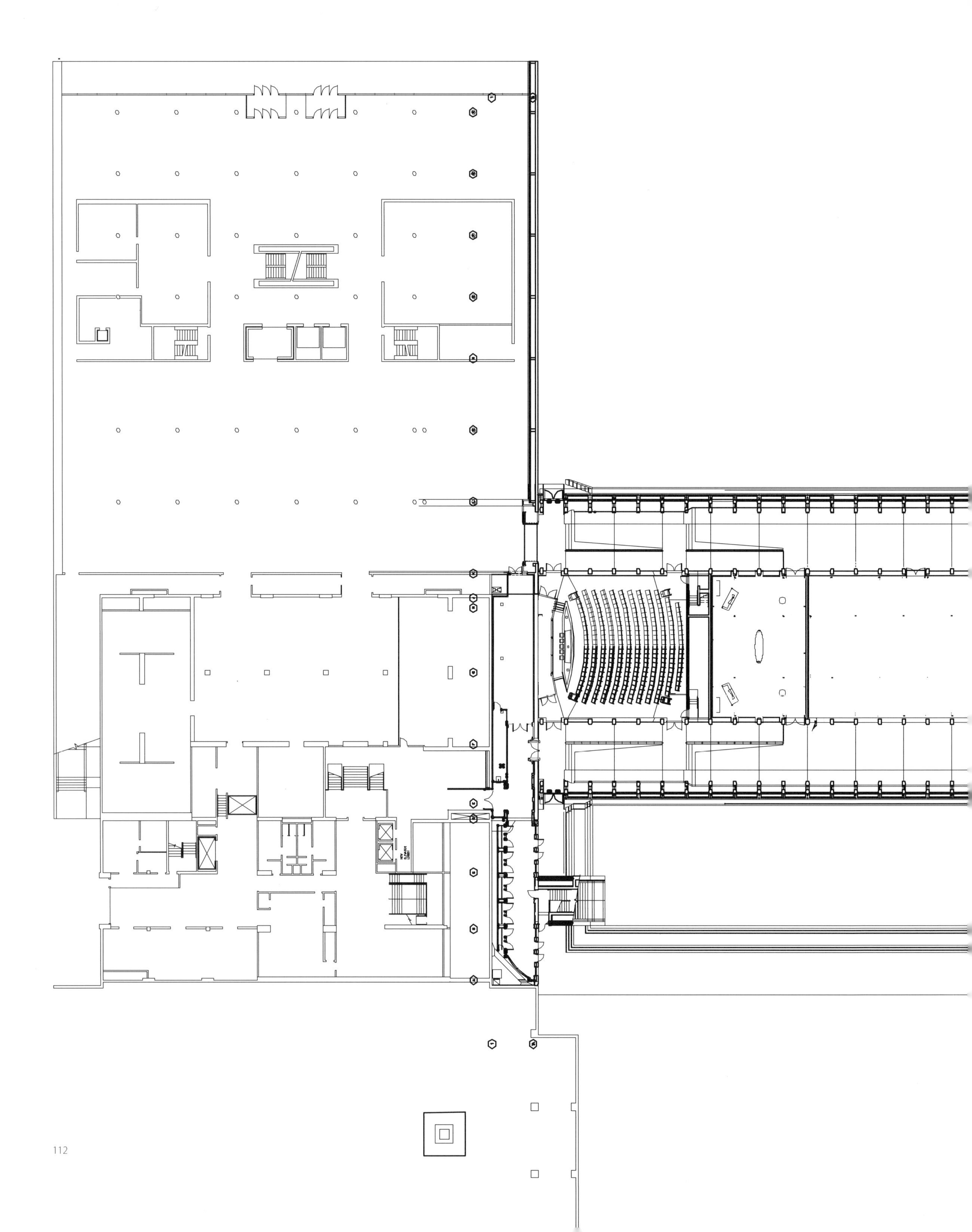

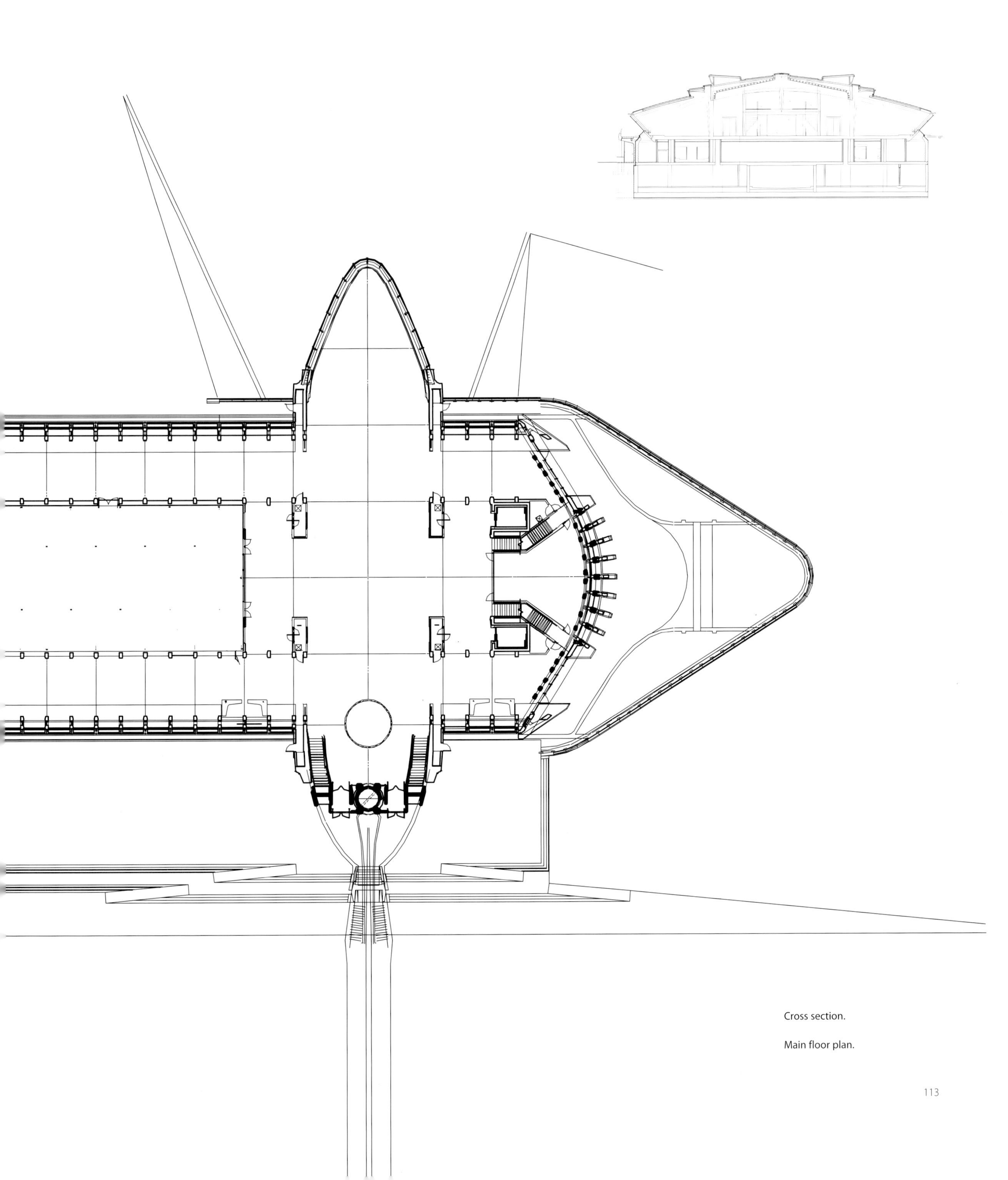

Cross section.

Main floor plan.

Santiago Calatrava: Biography

Santiago Calatrava

Architect, artist, and engineer Santiago Calatrava was born on July 28, 1951, in Valencia, Spain, and attended primary and secondary school there. From the age of eight he also attended the Arts and Crafts School, where he began his formal instruction in drawing and painting. When he was thirteen, his family took advantage of the recent opening of the borders and sent him to Paris as an exchange student. He later traveled and studied in Switzerland as well. Upon completing high school in Valencia, he went to Paris with the intention of enrolling in the Ecole des Beaux-Arts; but since he arrived in June 1968 at the height of student unrest, he found his plan was unworkable. He returned to Valencia and enrolled in the Escuela Tecnica Superior de Arquitectura, a relatively new institution, where he earned a degree in architecture and took a graduate course in urbanism. While at the school, he also undertook independent projects with a group of fellow students, producing two books on the vernacular architecture of Valencia and Ibiza.

Attracted by the mathematical rigor of certain great works of historic architecture, and feeling that his training in Valencia had given him no clear direction, Calatrava decided to pursue graduate studies in civil engineering, and he enrolled in 1975 at the Eidgenössische Technische Hochschule (ETH; the Federal Institute of Technology) in Zurich. He received his Ph.D. in 1979. It was during this period that he met and married his wife, who was a law student in Zurich. After completing his studies, Calatrava took a position as an assistant at the ETH and began to accept small engineering commissions, such as designing the roof for a library or the balcony of a private residence. He also began to enter competitions, believing that this was his most likely way to secure commissions. His first winning competition proposal, in 1983, was for the design and construction of the Stadelhofen Railway Station in Zurich, the city in which he established his office.

In 1984 Calatrava designed and built the Bach de Roda Bridge, commissioned for the Olympic Games in Barcelona. This was the beginning of the bridge projects that established his international reputation. Among the other notable bridges that followed were the Alamillo Bridge and La Cartuja Viaduct, commissioned for the World's Fair in Seville (1987–92); Campo Volantin pedestrian bridge in Bilbao (1990–97); and Alameda Bridge and Underground Station in Valencia (1991–95).

Calatrava established his firm's second office, in Paris, in 1989, when he was working on the Lyon Airport Railway Station (1989–94). He opened his third office, in Valencia, in 1991 to facilitate work on a competition, a very large cultural complex and urban intervention, the City of Arts and Sciences, Valencia (1991–2004). Other large-scale public projects from the late 1980s through the mid-1990s include the BCE Place mall in Toronto (1987–92); the Orient Station in Lisbon (1993–98, commissioned for Expo '98); and the winning proposal in the design competition to complete the Cathedral of St. John the Divine in New York (1991), a project that has not been realized.

Exhibitions of Calatrava's work were first mounted in 1985, with a showing of nine sculptures in an art gallery in Zurich. A new stage in recognition was marked by two solo exhibitions: a retrospective at the Royal Institute of British Architects, London, in 1992, and the exhibition *Structure and Expression* at the Museum of Modern Art, New York, in 1993. The latter exhibition included an installation in the museum's sculpture garden of *Shadow Machine*, a large-scale sculpture with undulating concrete "fingers." The most complete exhibition yet mounted of his work was *Santiago Calatrava: Artist, Architect, Engineer*, presented at the Palazzo Strozzi in Florence, Italy (2000–2001). Similar exhibitions were mounted in 2001 in Dallas, Texas (to inaugurate the new Meadows Museum at Southern Methodist University), and in Athens, at the National Gallery, Alexandros Soutzos Museum.

Major projects include the Sondica Airport, Bilbao (1990–2000); the Bridge of Europe, Orléans, France (1996–2000); the Bodegas Ysios Winery in Laguardia, Spain (1998–2001); James Joyce Bridge, Dublin, Ireland (1998–2003); the Tenerife Concert Hall, Santa Cruz, Canary Islands (1991–2003); the Petah Tikva Bridge, Tel Aviv, Israel (1998–2004); Piazzale Roma Footbridge, Venice, Italy (1996–2005); the Sundial Bridge at Turtle Bay Exploration Park in Redding, California (1995–2004); the Olympic Sports Complex in Athens (2001–4); and the Valencia Opera House (1996–2004), the last major building in his City of Arts and Sciences. Among his major recent commissions, Calatrava has been selected to design Symphony Center for the Atlanta Symphony Orchestra in Atlanta, Georgia, and the World Trade Center Transportation Hub in New York.

Honors and awards given to Santiago Calatrava include the Gold Medal of the Institute of Structural Engineers, London; the City of Toronto Urban Design Award; designation as a Global Leader for Tomorrow by the World Economic Forum in Davos; the Creu de Sant Jordi, Barcelona; the Gold Medal for Merit in the Fine Arts, Ministry of Culture, Granada, Spain; membership in Les Arts et Lettres, Paris; the Gold Medal of the Círculo de Bellas Artes, Valencia; Time magazine's "Best of 2001" designation for the expansion of the Milwaukee Art Museum; the Sir Misha Black Medal, Royal College of Art, London; the Leonardo da Vinci Medal, Société pour la Formation des Ingénieurs; and the Principe de Asturias Art Prize; the Gold Medal of Architecture of L'Académie d'Architecture, Paris; the Silver Beam Award of the Swedish Institute of Steel Construction; and the Illuminating Design Award of Merit of the Illuminating Engineering Society of North America, New York. He was awarded the 2005 Gold Medal from the American Institute of Architects, its highest award. In addition, Santiago Calatrava has received twelve honorary doctorates from universities in England, Israel, Italy, the Netherlands, Scotland, Spain, and the United States.

DANGER

Santiago Calatrava: Selected Projects and Works

Acleta Alpine Motor Bridge, Disentis, Switzerland, 1979 (project)

Roof for the IBA Squash Hall, Berlin, Germany, 1979 (competition project)

Letten Motorway Bridge, Zurich, Switzerland, 1982 (competition project)

Schwarzhaupt Factory, Dielsdorf, Switzerland, 1982 (competition project)

Mühlenareal Library, Thun, Switzerland, 1982 (competition project)

Rhine Bridge, Diepoldsau, Switzerland, 1982 (competition project)

Jakem Steel Warehouse, Münchwilen, Switzerland, 1983–84

Ernsting Warehouse, Coesfeld-Lette, Germany, 1983–85

Stadelhofen Railway Station, Zurich, Switzerland, 1983–90

St. Fiden Bus Stop Shelter, St. Gall, Switzerland, 1983–85

Wohlen High School, Wohlen, Switzerland, 1983–88

Lucerne Station Hall, Lucerne, Switzerland, 1983–89

Bärenmatte Community Center, Suhr, Switzerland, 1984–88

Caballeros Footbridge, Lerida, Spain, 1984 (competition project)

Bach de Roda Bridge, Barcelona, Spain, 1984–87

9 d'Octubre Bridge, Valencia, Spain, 1986–88

St. Gall Youth Music School Concert Room, St. Gall, Switzerland, 1986

Blackbox Television Studio, Zurich, Switzerland, 1986–87

Tabourettli Theater, Basel, Switzerland, 1986–87

Raitenau Overpass, Salzburg, Austria, 1986 (competition project)

BCE Place Gallery and Heritage Square, Toronto, Canada, 1987–92

Oudry-Mesly Footbridge, Créteil-Paris, France, 1987–88

Pontevedra Bridge, Pontevedra, Spain, 1987 (project)

Basarrate Underground Station, Bilbao, Spain, 1987 (competition project)

Alamillo Bridge and La Cartuja Viaduct, Seville, Spain, 1987–92

Cascine Footbridge, Florence, Italy, 1987 (project)

Leimbach Footbridge and Station, Zurich, Switzerland, 1988 (competition project)

Lusitania Bridge, Mérida, Spain, 1988–91

Wettstein Bridge, Basel, Switzerland, 1988 (project)

Gentil Bridge, Paris, France, 1988 (competition project)

Emergency Services Center, St. Gall, Switzerland, 1988–98

Miraflores Bridge, Cordoba, Spain, 1989 (project)

Montjuic Communications Tower, Barcelona, Spain, 1989–92

Reuss Footbridge, Flüelen, Switzerland, 1989 (competition project)

Zurich University, Faculty of Law Library, Zurich, Switzerland, 1989–2004

Lyon Airport Railway Station, Satolas-Lyon, France, 1989–94

Gran Via Bridge, Barcelona, Spain, 1989 (competition project)

Puerto Bridge, Ondarroa, Spain, 1989–95

La Devesa Footbridge, Ripoll, Spain, 1989–91

Campo Volantin Footbridge, Bilbao, Spain, 1990–97

East London River Crossing, London, England, 1990 (project)

Sondica Airport, Bilbao, Spain, 1990–2000

Tenerife Concert Hall, Santa Cruz, Tenerife, Canary Islands, Spain, 1991–2003

Calabria Soccer Stadium, Calabria, Italy, 1991 (competition project)

City of Arts and Sciences, Communications Tower, Valencia, Spain, 1991 (competition project)

Kuwait Pavilion, Expo '92, Seville, Spain, 1991–92

Salou Soccer Stadium, Salou, Spain, 1991 (competition project)

City of Arts and Sciences, Museum and Planetarium, Valencia, Spain, 1991–2000

Alameda Bridge and Underground Station, Valencia, Spain, 1991–95

Cathedral of St. John the Divine, New York, New York, 1991 (competition project)

Kronprinzen Bridge, Berlin, Germany, 1991–96

Spandau Railway Station, Berlin, Germany, 1991 (competition project)

Médoc Swingbridge, Bordeaux, France, 1991 (competition project)

Klosterstrasse Railway Viaduct, Berlin, Germany, 1991 (project)

Jahn Olympic Sports Complex, Berlin, Germany, 1991 (competition project)

Solferino Footbridge, Paris, France, 1992 (competition project)

Tenerife Exhibition Center, Santa Cruz, Tenerife, Canary Islands, Spain, 1992–95

Reichstag Conversion, Berlin, Germany, 1992 (competition project)

Lake Bridge, Lucerne, Switzerland, 1992 (competition project)

Alcoy Community Hall, Plaza, and Fountain, Alcoy, Spain, 1992–95

Alcoy Bridge, Alcoy, Spain, 1992 (project)

Trinity Footbridge, Salford-Manchester, England, 1993–95

Orient Station, Lisbon, Portugal, 1993–98

St. Paul's Footbridge, London, England, 1994 (project)

Milwaukee Art Museum, Quadracci Pavilion, Milwaukee, Wisconsin, 1994–2001

Sundial Bridge, Redding, California, 1995–2004

Soccer Stadium, Marseille, France, 1995 (competition project)

Pont d'Orléans, Orléans, France, 1996–2000

City of Arts and Sciences, Opera House, Valencia, Spain, 1996–2004

Liège-Guillemins TGV Station, Liège, Belgium, 1996–2006

Observatory Bridge, Liège, Belgium, 1996–2000

Piazzale Roma Footbridge, Venice, Italy, 1996–2005

Barajas Airport, Madrid, Spain, 1997 (competition project)

Petah Tikva Footbridge, Tel Aviv, Israel, 1998–2004

Bodegas Ysios Winery, Laguardia, Spain, 1998–2001

Puerto Madero/Puente de la Mujer Footbridge, Buenos Aires, Argentina, 1998–2004

James Joyce Bridge, Dublin, Ireland, 1998–2003

Three Bridges over the Hoofdvaart Canal, Haarlemmermeer, the Netherlands, 1999–2004

Turning Torso Apartment Tower, Malmö, Sweden, 1999–2005

Olympic Sports Complex, Athens, Greece, 2001–4

Queens Landing Footbridge, Chicago, Illinois, 2001 (project)

Woodall Rodgers Extension Bridge, Dallas, Texas, 2002–

Symphony Center, Atlanta, Georgia, 2002–

Light Rail Train Bridge, Jerusalem, Israel, 2002–

World Trade Center Transportation Hub, New York, New York, 2003–

80 South Street Tower, New York, New York, 2003–

Selected Bibliography

Blaser, Werner, ed. *Santiago Calatrava: Engineering Architecture*. Basel and Boston: Birkhäuser, 1989. Contributions by Kenneth Frampton and Pierluigi Nicolin.

Calatrava, Santiago. *Dynamic Equilibrium: Recent Projects*. Exh. cat. Zurich: Verlag für Architektur, 1992.

———. *Santiago Calatrava*. Exh. cat. Madrid: El Croquis, 1993.

———. *Santiago Calatrava: Sculptures and Drawings*. Exh. cat. Madrid: Aldeasa, 2001. Contributions by Kosme de Barañano, Javier Arnaldo, and Antón Capitel.

———. *Structures in Movement: The Architecture of Santiago Calatrava*. Exh. cat. Dallas, Tex.: Meadows Museum, Southern Methodist University, 2001.

Cullen, Michael S., and Martin Kieren. *Calatrava, Berlin: Five Projects*. Basel and Boston: Birkhäuser, 1994.

Daniels, Klaus, ed. *Hohe Häuser: Kontroverse Beiträge zu einem unstrittenen Bautypus*. Stuttgart: Hatje, 1993.

Frampton, Kenneth, Anthony C. Webster, and Anthony Tischhauser. *Calatrava Bridges*. 3rd ed. Basel and Boston: Birkhäuser, 2004.

Harbison, Robert. *Creatures from the Mind of the Engineer: The Architecture of Santiago Calatrava*. Zurich: Artemis, 1992.

Jodidio, Philip. *Oriente Station*. Lisbon: Centralivros, 1998.

———. *Santiago Calatrava*. Cologne: Taschen, 1998; rev. ed. 2003.

Kausel, Cecilia Lewis, and Ann Pendleton-Jullian, eds. *Santiago Calatrava: Conversations with Students: The M.I.T. Lectures*. New York: Princeton Architectural Press, 2002.

Klein, Bernhard. *Santiago Calatrava: Bahnhof Stadelhofen, Zürich*. Tübingen and Berlin: Ernst Wasmuth, 1993.

Kiley, Dan, and Jane Amidon. *Dan Kiley: The Complete Works of America's Master Landscape Architect*. Boston: Little, Brown, 1999.

Levin, Michael. *Calatrava: Drawings and Sculptures*. Zurich: Santiago Calatrava Valls, 2000.

———. *Santiago Calatrava, the Artworks: A Laboratory of Ideas, Forms, and Structures*. Basel and Boston: Birkhäuser, 2003.

McQuaid, Matilda. *Santiago Calatrava: Structure and Expression*. Exh. cat. New York: Museum of Modern Art, 1993.

Milwaukee Art Museum. *Building a Masterpiece: Milwaukee Art Museum*. New York: Hudson Hills Press, 2001. Introduction by Russell Bowman; essay by Franz Schulze.

Molinari, Luca. *Santiago Calatrava*. Milan: Skira, 1999. Catalogue entries by Erika Samsa.

Nicolin, Pierluigi, and Marcel Meili. *The Daring Flight: Santiago Calatrava*. Milan: Electa, and New York: Rizzoli, 1987.

Polano, Sergio. *Santiago Calatrava: Complete Works*. Corte Madera, Calif.: Gingko, 1996.

Pollalis, Spiro N. *What is a Bridge? The Making of Calatrava's Bridge in Seville*. Cambridge, Mass.: MIT Press, 1999.

Seipel, Wilfried, ed. *Santiago Calatrava: Like a Bird*. Exh. cat. Milan: Skira, 2003.

Sharp, Dennis, ed. *Santiago Calatrava*. 2nd ed. London and New York: E & FN Spon and Book Art, 1994.

———. *Santiago Calatrava*. London: Academy Editions, 1996.

Tischhauser, Anthony, and Stanislaus von Moos, eds. *Calatrava: Public Buildings*. Basel and Boston: Birkhäuser, 1998.

Trame, Umberto, ed. *Santiago Calatrava: Quadracci Pavilion, Milwaukee Art Museum*. Bologna: Editrice Compositori, 2001.

Tzonis, Alexander. *Santiago Calatrava: The Poetics of Movement*. New York: Universe, 1999.

———. *Santiago Calatrava: The Complete Works*. New York: Rizzoli, 2004.

Tzonis, Alexander, and Liane Lefaivre. *Movement, Structure, and the Work of Santiago Calatrava*. Basel and Boston: Birkhäuser, 1995.

Tzonis, Alexander, and Liane Lefaivre, eds. *Santiago Calatrava's Creative Process*. 2 vols. Basel: Birkhäuser, 2001.

Zardini, Mirko, ed. *Santiago Calatrava: Secret Sketchbook*. New York: Monacelli Press, 1996.

Acknowledgments

I jumped at the chance to write this book because I wanted to think deeply about this architect and this building, admiring both as I already did. It has been as interesting as I had hoped. There were surprises: anyone who has written about architecture for as long as I have knows that it's rare for large-scale projects to end with all parties speaking to one another rather than through their attorneys. After the Milwaukee museum addition was finished, no one had a bad word to say about anyone. I prodded for the underlying conflict and viciousness and never found it. Astonishing. These are exceptional people who were working on an extraordinary project and they knew it. They gave it everything they had and they collaborated to get it done. (With the schedule set for this book, editor Robert Sharp and I have had a little taste of what the building team experienced.) I would like to thank Santiago Calatrava who counts among his gifts inspiring passionate commitment to architecture in other people. From the building team, I would like to thank David Kahler, Steve Chamberlin, and John Kissinger: all of these gentlemen were very helpful to me. Russell Bowman was similarly generous. Whitney Gould was kind enough to make corrections to my first draft. David Gordon, Robert Sharp, and Britt Salvesen enlisted me for the book and I will always be grateful for their support. In the course of interviewing building-team members, I often heard the lament, "I'll never work on anything this fun again." Well, my hope for all the people named here is that they—and I—get to work on projects this fun again, whether they are books or buildings.

CHERYL KENT
CHICAGO

Cheryl Kent has been writing about architecture for twenty years. Her work has appeared in the *New York Times*, *Architectural Record*, *Progressive Architecture*, *Metropolis*, *World Architecture*, and numerous other publications. She is the author of Rizzoli's *The Nature of Dwellings: The Architecture of David Hovey*.